WALKS FROM
WELSH HERITAGE RAILWAYS

Walks from
Welsh Heritage Railways

Dorothy Hamilton

ISBN: 0-86381-771-8

Cover design: Alan Jones

First published in 2002 by
Gwasg Carreg Gwalch, 12 Iard yr Orsaf, Llanrwst,
Wales LL26 0EH
☎ 01492 642031 🖷 01492 641502
✆ books@carreg-gwalch.co.uk   website: www.carreg-gwalch.co.uk

Contents

Location Map 7
Introduction 8
Railway Enquiries 9
Tourist Information Centres 9

RAILWAYS & WALKS

Vale of Rheidol Railway 10
Walk 1   Devil's Bridge (Pontarfynach) – Rheidol Falls –
           Cwm Rheidol Reservoir – Aber-ffrwd 12

Tal-y-llyn Railway 16
Walk 2   Tywyn – Afon Dysynni – Rhydyronnen 18
Walk 3   Dôl-goch Falls 22
Walk 4   Nant Gwernol – Abergynolwyn – Llanllwyda –
           Dôl-goch 25
Walk 5   Nant Gwernol – Bryneglwys Quarry –
           Abergynolwyn Station 29

Fairbourne & Barmouth Steam Railway 33
Walk 6   Fairbourne – Friog – Cyfannedd – Blue Lake –
           Fairbourne 35
Walk 7   Y Bermo (Barmouth) – Dinas Olau – Pont
           y Bermo – Fairbourne 39

Ffestiniog Railway 43
Walk 8   Minffordd – Portmeirion – Porthmadog 45
Walk 9   Tan-y-bwlch – Rhiw Goch – Penrhyndeudraeth –
           Minffordd 49
Walk 10 Tan-y-bwlch – Llyn Mair – Plas Halt –
           Llyn Hafod-y-llyn – Tan-y-bwlch 54
Walk 11 Y Dduallt – Coed-y-bleiddiau – Tan-y-bwlch 58
Walk 12 Y Dduallt – Tanygrisiau Reservoir – Afon
           Goedol – Y Dduallt 61
Walk 13 Tanygrisiau – Llyn Cwmorthin – Rhosydd –
           Tanygrisiau 82

Walk 14 Blaenau Ffestiniog – Tanygrisiau – Y Dduallt 86

Welsh Highland Railway 90
Walk 15 Waunfawr – Moel Smytho – Waunfawr 91

Trên Bach yr Wyddfa – Snowdon Mountain Railway 95
Walk 16 Snowdon Summit – Bwlch Glas – Halfway
         House – Llanberis 97

Great Orme Tramway 101
Walk 17 Great Orme – Country Park – Ffynnon
         Rufeiniog – Great Orme 103
Walk 18 Great Orme – Monk's Path – Llandudno 105

Llangollen Railway 109
Walk 19 Llangollen – Llangollen Canal – Castell Dinas
         Brân – Llangollen 111
Walk 20 Berwyn – Valle Crucis Abbey – Llangollen 115
Walk 21 Glyndyfrdwy – Dreboeth – Nant y
         Pandy – Glyndyfrdwy 119
Walk 22 Carrog – Nant-y-fadwen – Glyndyfrdwy 123
Walk 23 Carrog – Llidiart y Parc – Moel Fferna – Carrog ... 127

Rheilffordd Llyn Tegid 129
Walk 24 Bala – Bryniau Goleu – Llangower 131
Walk 25 Llangower – Cae'r Hafoty – Glyn Gower –
         Llangower 135

Welshpool & Llanfair Railway 138
Walk 26 Llanfair Caereinion 139

Location Map

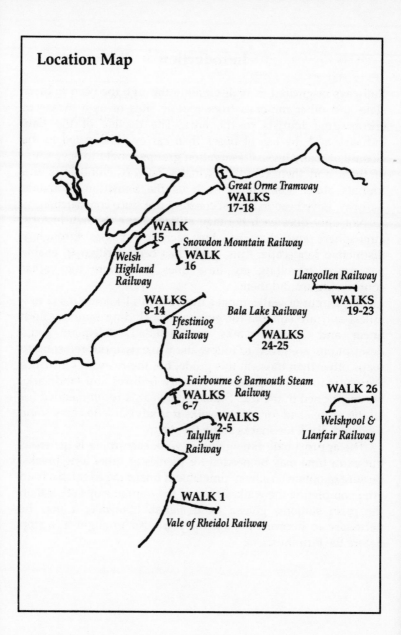

Great Orme Tramway
WALKS 17-18

WALK 15

Snowdon Mountain Railway
WALK 16

Welsh Highland Railway

Llangollen Railway
WALKS 19-23

WALKS 8-14

Ffestiniog Railway

Bala Lake Railway
WALKS 24-25

Fairbourne & Barmouth Steam Railway
WALKS 6-7

WALK 26

WALKS 2-5

Welshpool & Llanfair Railway

Talyllyn Railway

WALK 1

Vale of Rheidol Railway

Introduction

Railways originated in Wales mainly through the need to carry slate and other minerals from remote sites or as a means of encouraging tourists to the area. The decline of the slate industry and the use of buses then car ownership led to the closure of many lines. Preservation groups fought to save some of them and their rebirth fascinates railway enthusiasts and tourists alike. Some lines, such as the Snowdon Mountain Railway, have been in almost constant use since construction.

Not only does each heritage railway have its own history, atmosphere and character, but each line passes through a distinctive landscape. This guide has been written to enable passengers travelling on these lines to explore the varied countryside around them.

The length of walks ranges from 3.5 to 11 kilometres (2 to 7 miles) and are suitable for everyone, including families. Both linear and circular walks are included. Adequate route descriptions are given to follow the walks without referring to maps other than those in this guide, but the relevant Ordnance Survey map will help you to identify features and landmarks not mentioned in the text. Sturdy footwear is recommended for all the routes and for longer walks it is advisable to carry some food and drink for snacks along the way.

The approximate time given to walk each route is generous but extra time may be needed for picnics or other long breaks. Be sure to obtain a railway timetable if intending to catch a train after completing the walk. To board the train at stops other than the main stations, give a hand signal. Likewise, it may be necessary to inform the guard if you wish to alight at a stop before the terminus.

Railway Enquiries

Vale of Rheidol Railway	01970	625819
Tal-y-llyn Railway	01654	710472
Fairbourne & Barmouth Steam Railway	01341	250362
Ffestiniog Railway	01766	512340
Welsh Highland Railway	01766	512340
Snowdon Mountain Railway	01286	870223
Great Orme Tramway	01492	574003
Llangollen Railway	01978	860951
Bala Lake Railway	01678	540666
Welshpool & Llanfair Railway	01938	810441

Tourist Information Centres

Aberystwyth	01970	612125
Tywyn	01654	710070
Y Bermo (Barmouth)	01341	280787
Porthmadog	01766	512981
Blaenau Ffestiniog	01766	830360
Caernarfon	01286	672232
Llanberis	01286	870765
Llandudno	01492	876413
Llangollen	01978	860828
Bala	01678	521021
Welshpool	01938	552043

Vale of Rheidol Railway

Now one of the main tourist attractions in the Aberystwyth area, the Vale of Rheidol Railway was constructed to carry ore from the lead mines in Cwm Rheidol to the coast. Building of the 1ft 11½inch (597mm) gauge railway started in 1901 and a year later freight traffic was carried on the line. Passenger trains started on 22 December 1902. At first it was owned by a private company but it was taken over by the Cambrian Railway in 1923, which was taken over by the Great Western Railway.

During the 1914-18 war the railway carried timber from the forests of Cwm Rheidol for use in coal mines in South Wales. Later, the service deteriorated owing to the decline in the mines that used the line and goods operations ceased in 1927. Bus services took away passenger traffic and in 1931 the line stopped its winter schedule. From then on, the railway was run mainly for tourists. Services were suspended during the Second World War and in 1948 the line was taken over by British Railways. It was the last steam railway run by British Rail until the owners of the Brecon Mountain Railway purchased it in 1989.

Two of the substantial locomotives, No. 7 *Owain Glyndŵr* and No. 8 *Llywelyn*, were built at Swindon in 1923 to designs similar to the first locos that operated on the line. No. 9 *Prince of Wales* has been built from the engine called No. 2 *Prince of Wales* that was built for the railway by Davis and Metcalfe of Manchester in 1902. Because the line runs through a thickly forested area, all the locomotives have been converted to burn oil to minimise the risk of fire.

On the journey of 19 km (12 miles) from Aberystwyth to Pontarfynach (Devil's Bridge), the train rises over 180 metres (600 ft). The climb is 1 in 50 for much of the way from Aberffrwd to Pontarfynach, and offers superb views of Cwm Rheidol.

Trains run most days from Easter to late October.

Exceptions, when trains may not be running, are Fridays and Sundays at the beginning and end of the season. Extra trains operate during peak holiday periods.

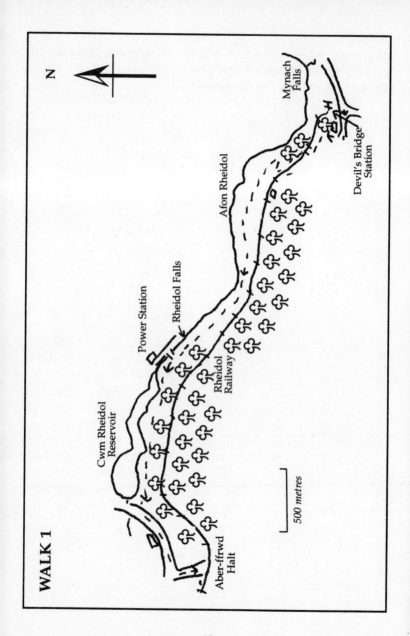

WALK 1

N

Mynach Falls

Devil's Bridge Station

Afon Rheidol

Power Station

Rheidol Falls

Cwm Rheidol Reservoir

Rheidol Railway

500 metres

Aber-ffrwd Halt

12

Pontarfynach (Devil's Bridge) – Rheidol Falls – Cwm Rheidol Reservoir – Aber-ffrwd

Route: A long descent through woodland is followed by easy level walking through Cwm Rheidol.

Start: Vale of Rheidol Railway, Devil's Bridge Station (Pontarfynach).

Finish: Aber-ffrwd Station.

Facilities: Refreshments and toilets at the start.

Time: 3½ hours.

OS Maps: 1:50 000 Landranger 135;
                 1:25 000 Explorer 213.

At Devil's Bridge, Afon Mynach joins Afon Rheidol by plunging over 100 metres in a series of waterfalls. Afon Mynach is spanned by three bridges built directly above one another. The lowest, a simple medieval stone bridge, was probably built by the monks of Strata Florida Abbey *(Ystrad Fflur)* to gain access to sheep pasture. According to legend, the Devil built the bridge in return for the first living thing to cross it, but he was thwarted in his desire for a woman's soul when her dog scampered across the bridge ahead of her. In the 16th century, some thieves and murderers known as *plant de bat* (bat children – two brothers and a sister) lived in a cave below the gorge. Eventually, they were hanged at Rhayader. The second, wider bridge was built in the 18th century and above it is a modern road bridge. The footpaths to view the falls are quite strenuous and there is an admission charge. The route does not pass the entrance to the falls so if you wish to visit them before following the walk, turn left when leaving the station.

Oak and coniferous woodland clothe the steep sides of beautiful Cwm Rheidol, part of which is a nature reserve. In the early 20th century, lead mining took place in the valley and the ore was taken out by train. The walk passes the Rheidol Falls and fish ladder from where a diversion can be made to the Rheidol Power Station Visitor Centre. A wide variety of birds may be seen on the walk.

Walk Directions:

1. From Devil's Bridge Station walk out to the road and turn right. Ignore the road on the left to Tregaron and pass bungalows on the right. At the end of the last garden, turn right through a field gate.

2. Walk ahead and pass trees on the left. At arrows, before the bottom of the field, turn left to follow a path above the railway line. Ignore a right-hand fork and, in another 150 metres, go through a small gate. Walk beside a fence and the railway line. Climb over a stile and bear left a few metres before crossing the line to a narrow path.

3. Follow the path through the woods to a stile. Cross the line again and proceed with a fence and the line on your right. Cross another stile and the line to another path. It descends the hill gradually by bending first to the right and then left, before making a long descent through trees to a forest track. Maintain your direction, downhill.

4. On reaching a notice for Coed Rheidol National Nature Reserve near a gate, turn left uphill to a corner fence. Walk along with the fence on your right to a path junction. Bear right to follow a fairly level path. Go through a couple of gates and ignore a path on the left going uphill. Continue beside a fence and cross a stile.

5. Follow the fence for about 100 metres above mine buildings

then bear right downhill into the field. Walk ahead close to Afon Rheidol to a weir. Cross a stile onto an enclosed path. There are two stiles on the left but, for a good view of Rheidol Falls, walk a short way across the footbridge. (To visit the Power Station, cross the footbridge and bear left for 250 metres.)

6. Return to the stiles and cross the one nearest the river. Walk uphill a few paces but soon slant right to a post with an arrow. From the post go left about five metres then bear right to cross a meadow. Walk towards a line of trees. Cross the old field boundary and follow a line of trees on your left, and then on your right. Continue ahead below the hill and shortly follow a clear path uphill for a few paces. The path levels and runs above the river to a stile.

7. Ignore paths leading off to the left and walk ahead to another stile. Continue on a clear path and emerge on a track. Bear right to have Cwm Rheidol Reservoir and its dam on your right. Follow the track to some gates and emerge on a lane. The walk turns left here but, before finishing the walk, you may like to bear right 100 metres to the bridge and its viewpoints of the nearby weir.

8. Return along the lane and walk uphill to a lane junction. Turn left uphill and in 150 metres, a few paces before a level crossing, bear right through a gate to Aber-ffrwd Halt.

Tal-y-llyn Railway

Tal-y-llyn Railway originated from the need to transport slate from the Bryneglwys Quarry in the hills above Abergynolwyn to the coast. Prior to its construction, slate had been carried by packhorse to Aberdyfi for shipment. This was a costly and laborious form of transport and when the Aberdyfi Slate Company Ltd. took over the quarry, James Spooner of Ffestiniog was appointed to engineer a 10.5 km (6½ mile) line from Tywyn to Abergynolwyn. Permission for the construction of the 2ft 3inch (686mm) gauge was given in 1865. The locomotives used on the line were *Tal-y-llyn* and *Dôl-goch*, which were built by Fletcher Jennings and Co. of Whitehaven. Slate was transported to a station near the sidings of the main line station at Tywyn but the passenger service, which began in 1866, terminated for some years at Pendre on the eastern side of the town. A donkey was stabled there to carry people's luggage to the main line station.

In 1911, the railway and quarry were bought by Tywyn businessman and Liberal MP, Sir Henry Haydn Jones. As the slate industry declined, the tourist traffic became more important. The quarry closed in 1947, but Sir Haydn managed to keep the railway going although it was, by this time, in a poor state of repair. After his death in 1950 it was suggested that a voluntary society ran the railway on a non-profit making basis. A year later, headed by L.T.C. Rolt, the Tal-y-llyn Railway Preservation Society was formed. It was the first of its kind.

One of the aims of the society was to extend the line along the old tramway and this was achieved in 1976. *Tal-y-llyn* and *Dôl-goch* have been joined by several more locomotives, including *Sir Haydn* and *Edward Thomas* from the Corris Railway. Another name for 'Edward' is 'Peter Sam', of the Rev'd W. Awdrey's books. His friend Duncan is *Douglas*, a loco that was built at Kilmarnock and operated at RAF Calshot for many years before coming to the Tal-y-llyn Railway. Locomotive *Tom Rolt* hauled turf for the Irish Turf Board *(Bord na Mona)* before being rebuilt at Pendre.

Trains operate daily from April to early November. They also run for a week starting on Boxing Day and on a few days in February and March. There are also a number of special events. Tickets issued include day rovers and eight day runabouts with unlimited travel from any station.

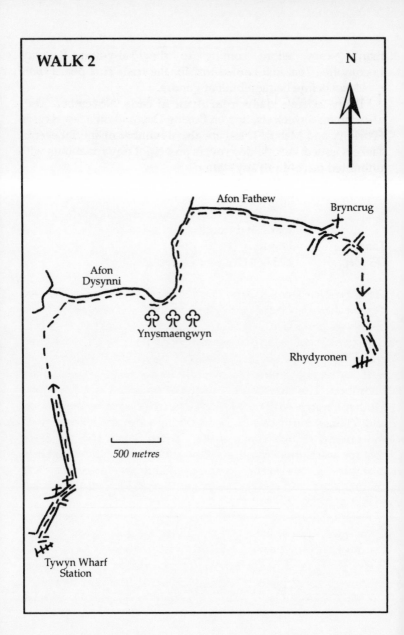

WALK 2

N

Afon Fathew

Bryncrug

Afon
Dysynni

Ynysmaengwyn

Rhydyronen

500 metres

Tywyn Wharf
Station

Tywyn – Afon Dysynni – Bryncrug – Rhydyronnen

Route: Easy level riverside walking and field paths.
Start: Tal-y-llyn Railway Wharf Station, Tywyn.
Finish: Rhydyronnen Station.
Facilities: Railway museum and refreshments at the start.
                  Pub in Bryncrug. Toilets at Tywyn Wharf, near
                  St Cadfan's Church and Bryncrug. Camp site
                  near Rhydyronnen.
Time: 3 hours.
OS Map: 1:25 000 Outdoor Leisure 23.

From being a small village lying some distance from the sea, Tywyn has expanded into a town and seaside resort. The history of the place dates back from the 6th century when St Cadfan and his brothers arrived from Brittany. They settled around a well close to the present high street. Others were attracted to the simple life of study, prayer and growing their own food. The church grew over the centuries to become the Mother Church of the area. Early churches were built of wood and Vikings burnt two of them. Dating from the 12th century, the present church contains the Cadfan Stone and the 5-7th century inscriptions on it are thought to be the oldest written examples of the Welsh language. There are also two 14th century effigies. One, known as the Crying Knight, sheds tears in wet weather.

From the church, the walk continues to Afon Dysynni, a good place for watching birds such as ducks and herons. Cormorants may be seen flying inland to Craig y Deryn (Bird Rock). After leaving the river, the path arrives at the village of Bryncrug, burial place of Mary Jones. In 1800, at the age of 16, she walked from Llanfihangel-y-Pennant to Bala to buy a Welsh

Bible from Mr Thomas Charles, a Methodist minister. Impressed by her determination, and realising there was a great need for Bibles, he persuaded the Religious Tract Society to establish the British and Foreign Bible Society. Mary later married and lived at Bryncrug. She is buried in the graveyard of Capel Bethlehem.

Walk Directions:

1. From Tal-y-llyn Railway Wharf Station walk out to the road and bear slightly right to cross the A493. Go along Neptune Road to where it emerges at a small roundabout with a memorial. Turn right and, in a few metres, ignore a road on the right. Pass the English Presbyterian Church and the Church of St Cadfan on your left.

2. Immediately after passing St Cadfan's Church turn left along Gwalia Road. After passing houses, the road continues straight ahead in the direction of Afon Dysynni.

3. Go through a gate across the road and, in another 200 metres, ignore a footbridge on the left at a footpath signpost. Continue ahead through a kissing-gate to another signpost. Bear half-right to cross the field and go through a gate into another field. Walk on to a stile near the right corner.

4. Go up to the embankment. On your left is Broad Water and, a few miles distant, to your right is Craig y Deryn. Bear right to have Afon Dysynni on your left. Pass trees at Ynysmaengwyn and ignore footpaths on your right.

5. After walking along the embankment for about 2 kilometres you will arrive at the point where a narrower river, Afon Fathew, flows into Afon Dysynni. Bear right with the path to have Afon Fathew on your left. Follow it to the A493 in Bryncrug.

6. Cross the road and turn left. Almost immediately, bear right in the direction of Tal-y-llyn. Pass a bus stop and, in a few metres, you will see a ladder stile on your right. (At Capel Bethlehem, further along this road, is Mary Jones's grave.)

7. After crossing the stile, turn left to have the river on your right. Pass behind the chapel and walk through a field. Go through a gap in a hedge and follow the river to a footbridge. Walk ahead to a kissing-gate but do not go through it. Turn left on a path and, after passing a house on the right, cross a bridge and follow a drive to a road.

8. Cross directly to another road. In about 50 metres, climb a stile on the right and follow a path into a field. Walk beside the left boundary to the next stile. Continue along the right side of the field to a stile and gate. Follow a stream on your right to a footbridge and stone stile. Turn left to Rhydyronnen Station.

WALK 3

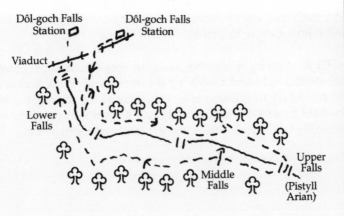

Dôl-goch Falls Station

Dôl-goch Falls Station

Viaduct

Lower Falls

Middle Falls

Upper Falls (Pistyll Arian)

500 metres

Walk 3   2 miles (3.2 kilometres)

Dôl-goch Falls Station – Lower Falls – Upper Falls – Dôl-goch Falls Station

Route: Paths through attractive woodland visit viewpoints of three waterfalls. Some sections are steep and may be slippery when wet.

Start/Finish: Tal-y-llyn Railway, Dôl-goch Falls Station.

Facilities: Tea Room at Dôl-goch Falls Hotel. Toilets at the station.

Time: 1½-2 hours.

OS Map: 1:25 000 Outdoor Leisure 23.

Accessible only by footpath or train and located in woodlands, the station at Dôl-goch makes a fine starting point for visiting the Dôl-goch Falls. A feature of interest here is the three arch railway viaduct that spans the nearby ravine. The Lower Falls are close by and from there a footpath climbs the tree-clad slope to the Middle and Upper Falls. Keep a look-out for woodland birds such as pied flycatchers. Where the stream flows placidly between the falls you may see dippers bobbing on rocks mid-stream.

Walk Directions:

1. At Dôl-goch Falls Station ignore the Way Out sign and walk on a few paces to a wide path signed 'To the Falls'. Pass picnic tables and cross a footbridge over the line. Walk down the railed path, which has a fine view of the railway viaduct.

2. On reaching the river, turn left through a kissing-gate. A viewing platform permits a good view of the Lower Falls. Walk back towards the gate but, before reaching it, bear right uphill

on a stepped path. Take either path at a fork to pass Twll yr Ogof and continue with the river on your right. To follow the full walk, do not cross any bridges before reaching the Upper Falls.

3. The path eventually ascends the hill by a series of zigzags from which a seat offers views of the Middle Falls. At a junction bear right to reach the Upper Falls (Pistyll Arian).

4. Cross the footbridge over the river. (If it is closed for any reason, return by your outward route.) Follow the path through the woods and ignore paths leading off it. Eventually you will drop down to the riverbank at a point just beyond the Lower Falls. Cross the footbridge and turn right to retrace your steps to the station. Or, for refreshments, turn left to the Dôl-goch Hotel and Tea Room.

Walk 4   6 miles (9.5 kilometres)

Nant Gwernol – Abergynolwyn – Llanllwyda – Dôl-goch

Route: Hillside paths and tracks with a long, gentle
                climb from Dyffryn Dysynni (valley), bypassing
                Craig y Deryn.
Start: Tal-y-llyn Railway, Nant Gwernol Station.
Finish: Dôl-goch Falls Station.
Facilities: Pub in Abergynolwyn. Tea Room at Dôl-goch
                Falls Hotel. Public toilets in Abergynolwyn.
                Camp site at Llanllwyda.
Time: 3½-4 hours.
OS Map: 1:25 000 Outdoor Leisure 23.

Abergynolwyn lies in the valley below the terminus of the Tal-y-llyn Railway. Before the 1860s, it did not exist as a village but consisted of two hamlets, Pandy and Cwrt. On the development of the Bryneglwys Quarry, the company built about seventy houses in three streets. A branch from the Tal-y-llyn Railway brought coal and provisions to the houses. There was a bakery in Pandy Square (now the car park) where villagers could take their own dough to be baked. In spring, fairs were held in the square. On the far side of Afon Dysynni, Cwrt dates back to the Middle Ages.

In Dyffryn Dysynni, the route passes Ty'n-y-bryn where the lexiographer William Owen Pughe was born in 1759. He spent much of his life in London and is best known for his Welsh and English Dictionary. On leaving the valley, the walk passes east of Craig y Deryn, the only inland nesting place of cormorants in the British Isles.

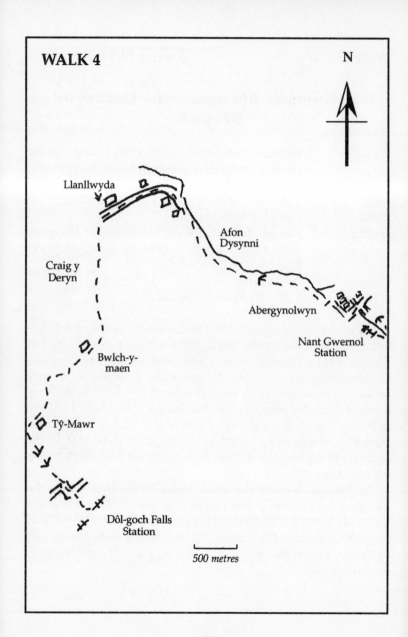

WALK 4

N

Llanllwyda

Craig y
Deryn

Afon
Dysynni

Abergynolwyn

Nant Gwernol
Station

Bwlch-y-
maen

Tŷ-Mawr

Dôl-goch Falls
Station

500 metres

Walk Directions:

1. From Nant Gwernol station follow the path to the bridge over Nant Gwernol. After crossing the bridge, bear left and ignore a path going uphill on the right. Walk along with the river on your left until the path veers right and emerges on a lane.

2. Turn left, downhill, and follow the lane to crossroads in Abergynolwyn. Turn left and pass the Railway Inn on your right. Pass a playground and immediately turn right. In 150 metres bear left to cross a footbridge over Nant Gwernol.

3. Walk ahead along the left boundary of the field before bearing right to pass buildings. Follow a fairly clear level path above trees to a ladder stile. After passing directly above the river, the path rises a little to cross the open hillside. In just over a kilometre it descends to the river again. On reaching a house, go through the right-hand gate and walk downhill to emerge on a lane.

4. Ignore the bridge on the right and walk ahead along the lane, which soon bends left. Craig y Deryn is soon visible ahead. After following the lane for just over a kilometre, you will pass Llanllwyda Farm on the right. In another 100 metres (where the lane bends right) cross a ladder stile on the left.

5. Walk uphill to a track and bear left. Continue beside a wall. Ignore a path on the right and go through a gate. Follow the clear green track uphill through the field to another gate (be sure to look back at the views). Continue uphill with a wall nearby on the left. In about 100 metres, bear left through a gap (where there was once a gate) and cross the field to a stile.

6. Follow a clear track to emerge on a farm access track. Turn

right and ignore a footpath on the left. Pass a house (Bwlch-y-maen) on the right. Pass through some gates and ignore a track on the right. Follow the track uphill beside a wall then descend to Ty-mawr Farm.

7. Pass the farmhouse on your left and walk downhill along the access lane. In about 100 metres cross a stile on the left. Follow the right boundary of two fields, crossing stiles. Veer slightly left to the next stile and cross a rocky hill. Walk downhill to follow a fence on the right. Before reaching the bottom of the field veer left, still descending, to find a path through bracken. It runs above the road. Cross a stile onto the B4405.

8. Turn left along the road and, where it bends left, go ahead on a track to pass the Dôl-goch Falls Hotel and Tea Room on your left. Go through a gate and bear left to Dôl-goch Falls Station.

Walk 5   *4 miles (6.5 kilometres)*

Nant Gwernol Station – Bryneglwys Quarry –
Abergynolwyn Station

Route:	A gradual climb to the disused Bryneglwys Quarry is followed by a descent along the old tramway and forest tracks and paths to Abergynolwyn Station.
Start:	Tal-y-llyn Railway, Nant Gwernol Station.
Finish:	Abergynolwyn Station.
Facilities:	Tea Room and toilets at Abergynolwyn Station.
Time:	3 hours.
OS Map:	1:25 000 Outdoor Leisure 23.

Bryneglwys quarry was first worked in the 1840s by John Pughe. In 1865, Lancashire cotton mill owners bought the quarry and developed it on a large scale building mills, inclines, tramways and the Tal-y-llyn Railway. At one time the quarry provided employment for three hundred men, but production slowed down in the early 20th century. Sir Haydn Jones bought the quarry and Tal-y-llyn Railway and there was a small boom in the 1920s. However, the 1939-45 war and lack of investment brought about its closure in 1947. Most of the structures have been demolished. At the former mill site there were several buildings including the manager's house, weighhouse, smithy, carpenters' shop and barracks for the men who lived too far away to commute everyday. They returned home for the weekends, Friday night to Monday morning. A tramway carried the slate from the quarry almost as far as Abergynolwyn Station. It ran from the mill to the top of the Beudynewydd incline and from its foot to the Cantrybedd cottages and another incline. It then passed above Nant Gwernol before descending the Allt-wyllt incline and continuing to the Tal-y-

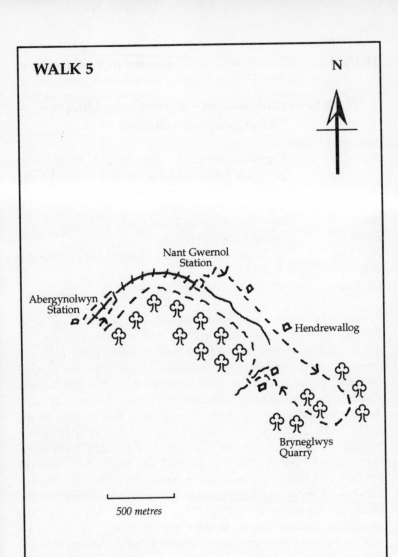

WALK 5

N

Nant Gwernol
Station

Abergynolwyn
Station

Hendrewallog

Bryneglwys
Quarry

500 metres

llyn Railway. A fine drumhouse still perches on a ledge above the Allt-wyllt incline. The weight of a loaded truck descending by gravity was used to raise the empty ones by means of cables and brakes.

Walk Directions:

1. At Nant Gwernol station walk along the platform to the end of the line. Ignore a path on the right and walk on above the river. Cross a footbridge and bear left but, in a few paces, turn right on a stepped path. At the top of the steps, leave the river by bearing left on another path, uphill. Ignore a path through trees on the right and follow the main path to a kissing-gate next to a broad gate.

2. Turn right along a lane. Beyond a gate across it, the lane passes above a stream and gives fine views over the valley. Ignore stiles on the right and note a ruin above on the left. Ahead is Tarren Hendre, the highest peak (634m) of the Tarren range. The lane passes below another ruin, Hendrewallog. In about another 400 metres, at a fork, take the right-hand level track, that runs beside a right-hand fence.

3. The track passes the Beudynewydd incline and goes through a gate to follow the old tramway. Pass a deep pit and ignore a footpath on the left. Climb a stile at a gate and walk through a flat area, formerly the site of the mill and other buildings for the Bryneglwys Quarry. Above on the left are more inclines and pits.

4. Pass a monkey puzzle tree and follow the track downhill through trees. When the track bends to the left, ignore a track on the right but, in another 20 metres, take the next track on the right. Pass between the ruined Cantrybedd cottages and cross a footbridge over Nant Moelfre.

5. Turn right to follow a path beside the stream. Ignore another footbridge near the foot of the Cantrybedd incline. Continue along a level path (the old horse tramway). Pass below the Alltwyllt drumhouse and descend a stepped path to a fork. (Here go right downhill if you wish to return to Nant Gwernol station.)

6. For Abergynolwyn station, ignore the right-hand path and continue through larch trees. Join a track and walk ahead. After passing a barrier, turn right and cross the line of the Tal-y-llyn Railway. Turn left on a path and follow it to Abergynolwyn Station.

Fairbourne and Barmouth Steam Railway

The line originated in the late 18th century as a 3.6 km (2 mile) 2ft (610mm) gauge horse-drawn tramway. Owned by Sir Arthur McDougall, the miller, its purpose was to carry building materials for use in the construction of the seaside village of Fairbourne. As building work came to an end, a horse-drawn passenger service was provided to link Fairbourne Station on the Cambrian Line with the ferry from Penrhyn Point to Barmouth.

In 1916, the tramway was taken over by Narrow Gauge Railways Ltd. and they reduced the gauge to 1ft 3inch (380mm) and introduced steam traction. The first locomotive, called *Prince Edward of Wales*, was built by Bassett-Lowke of Northampton. Another famous loco, *Count Louis*, was bought from Count Louis Zborowski, a Polish enthusiast who live at Highams, near Canterbury. The line changed hands several times but, after some prosperity, it started to deteriorate and operations ceased between 1939 and 1945. The area was used for military training, and this with drifting sands and floods caused much damage to the railway line.

After the war it was bought by business men from the Midlands and they relaid the line. *Count Louis*, after re-servicing, was joined by new steam and diesel locomotives. The line, known simply as the Fairbourne Railway (previously it was called Fairbourne Miniature Railway) operated successfully and had request stops at Bathing Beach and Golf Club Halts.

More changes came in 1985 under new ownership and the name was changed to Fairbourne and Barmouth Steam Railway. The track was relaid to 12¼inch (310mm) gauge. *Count Louis* and most of the other locos were sold. New locomotives include *Beddgelert* and *Southern* (Yeo). Golf Club Halt was renamed Gorsafawddachaidraigddanheddogleddollonpenrhyn areurdraethceredigion (the longest name of a station in Wales) which translates as The Mawddach station and its Dragon's teeth on the northerly Penrhyn drive on the golden beach of Cardigan Bay. Dragon's teeth was the term used locally in the 1939-45 war for the tank traps placed on the beach.

Trains run daily from Easter to the end of September and for a week at the school half-term in October. From April to September, weather and tides permitting, trains connect with a ferry service to and from Barmouth. Train tickets can be bought at both Fairbourne and Porth (Point) Penrhyn.

Walk 6   *4 miles (6.5 kilometres)*

Fairbourne – Friog – Cyfannedd Fawr – Blue Lake – Fairbourne

Route: A gradual ascent along hillside paths and tracks into the foothills above the Afon Mawddach estuary is followed by a descent past the Blue Lake.

Start/Finish: Fairbourne (steam) Railway Station.

Facilities: Cafe and toilets at the start. Museum and Nature Centre. Camp site nearby.

Time: 3-3½ hours.

OS Map: 1:25 000 Outdoor Leisure 23.

At the end of the 19th century, the building of the Cambrian Railway attracted wealthy industrialists to the Mawddach estuary. The miller Arthur McDougall bought land on the coastal plain near the village of Friog and built the holiday resort of Fairbourne. Local quarries also benefited from the coming of the Cambrian Railway as previously slate had to be carted a long distance to shipping points on Afon Mawddach. One such quarry was Goleuwern, passed on the walk. Opened in 1865 and worked for fifty years, it was never really successful. At first a hillside quarry, it was later developed as a pit, which is now flooded and known as the Blue Lake. The blue colour is caused by light reflected from the surrounding walls of the quarry. It is accessed by a short tunnel which divides in two before reaching the pool. Goleuwern's other remaining features include some impressive stone archways.

Walk Directions:

1. From the Fairbourne and Barmouth Railway Station, turn

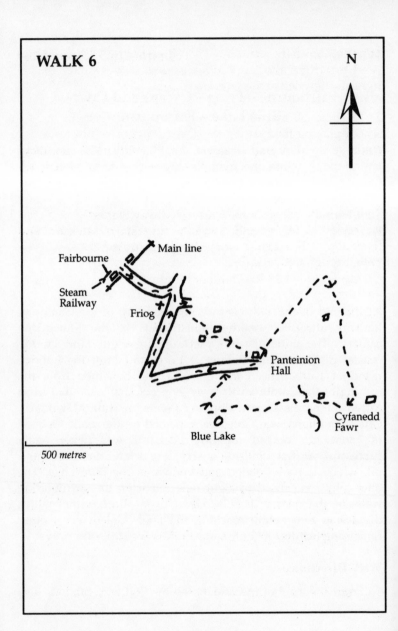

WALK 6

N

Fairbourne
Main line
Steam
Railway
Friog
Panteinion
Hall
Cyfanedd
Fawr
Blue Lake

500 metres

right and cross the main line's level crossing. On reaching the A493 turn right into the village of Friog. Pass a garage on the right and turn left along Ffordd yr Ysgol.

2. In about 50 metres turn right along a footpath to have a school playing field on the left. Go through a kissing-gate and continue beside a fence. Follow a path uphill through a field and in the direction of houses. Pass between them and bear left through a kissing-gate.

3. Ignore the access track and walk ahead to pass a long barn on the left. A few paces beyond it, veer right to walk below a fence and wall. When the fence bends left uphill, continue on a path through trees and descend to a gate and lane.

4. Turn left and follow the lane when it bears left to Panteinion Hall. Before reaching the entrance gates, turn right on a track to go through a kissing-gate. In 50 metres, at a fork, stay on the lower path, alongside a fence. Leave it in about 600 metres to take a higher path on the right.

5. Go through a gate and bear slightly left along the main track to pass above a cottage. Keep left at a fork and pass through a gap in a wall. Be sure to look back for fine views over Barmouth (*Y Bermo*). Go through another gap and continue along the partly walled track.

6. A few metres before reaching the farm buildings of Cyfannedd Fawr, turn right to have a wall on your right. Go through a gap in a wall and bear slightly left to the corner of the field. Now bear right and pass through a gap in the wall.

7. Walk ahead and, after crossing a stream, veer slightly right. At a ruin, bear left to pass it closely on your right. In about 40 metres go up a waymarked post and walk through trees to

another. Bear left to a kissing-gate and ford a stream.

8. Take the path that veers away from the stream. Follow the path for about 150 metres to a fork at the end of woodland. Ignore the left-hand fork uphill and take the lower path. In 50 metres bear slightly left to reach a track.

9. Bear right downhill to a junction. Turn left and, in about 200 metres, you will see, on your left, the short tunnel to the Blue Lake.

10. On leaving the tunnel, turn left for about 30 metres before bearing right on a path that descends under bridges to a track. Turn left to the lane met earlier. Either turn right and retrace your steps along the footpath to Friog, or bear left on the lane to the A493 and turn right to Friog and your starting point.

Barmouth (Y Bermo) Harbour – Dinas Olau – Pont y Bermo (Barmouth Bridge) – Fairbourne

Route: After a short, steep climb to viewpoints above Barmouth *(Y Bermo)*, the walk is completely level along Pont y Bermo (Barmouth [toll] Bridge) and the estuary embankment.

Start: Barmouth Harbour. If starting from Fairbourne, take the steam railway to Penrhyn Point (Porth Penrhyn) then the ferry across Afon Mawddach. Check first that the ferry is running.

Finish: Fairbourne. Check steam railway and ferry times if returning to Y Bermo.

Facilities: Refreshments and toilets in Y Bermo, Fairbourne and at Porth Penrhyn.

Time: 3-3½ hours.

OS Map: 1:25 000 Outdoor Leisure 23.

Y Bermo (Barmouth) is a small seaside town situated at the mouth of the beautiful Afon Mawddach estuary. Once a busy port well-known for its ship-building and flannel exports, the resort grew on the coming of the Cambrian Railway in 1867. Close to the harbour is the medieval building called Tŷ-gwyn where conspiracies took place against Richard III. Tŷ-crwn, the circular building nearby, was built in the 1830s as a lock-up for drunks. It is divided in two, one section for men, the other for women.

On a headland above the town, Dinas Olau was the National Trust's first property. The stone seat commemorates the 100th anniversary of Mrs Talbot giving two hectares of land to the Trust in 1885. A philanthropist, she also gave some cottages to

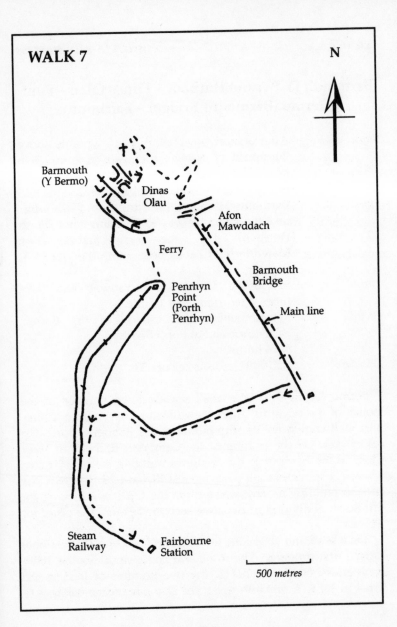

WALK 7

N

Barmouth
(Y Bermo)

Dinas
Olau

Afon
Mawddach

Ferry

Barmouth
Bridge

Penrhyn
Point
(Porth
Penrhyn)

Main line

Steam
Railway

Fairbourne
Station

500 metres

the writer and socialist John Ruskin who set up the Guild of St George. One of the tenants was the Frenchman Auguste Guyard and he encouraged local people to cultivate their gardens. He died in 1883.

Pont y Bermo offers magnificent views of the Afon Mawddach estuary. During excavations for the foundations, drilling revealed that the rock floor of the valley was actually 37 metres (120 feet) below alluvial deposits. Originally the section of the viaduct near the toll house had an overdraw bridge which could be rolled back to allow the passage of ships. Later, it was replaced by a swing bridge. In 1937, the bridge was used in a set of the film called 'The Ghost Train' in which a train is seen to fall from the open end of the viaduct into the sea. More recently, marine boring worms infested some timber piles of the structure, which have been replaced.

Walk Directions:

1. With your back to the harbour, turn left and pass the Bath House Cafe. A little distance to your right is Tŷ-crwn. Walk past the breakwater and, in another 200 metres, take a road on the right. Go over the level crossing and cross another road. Walk ahead to the main road.

2. Turn right and cross the road at the traffic lights. Bear right a few metres then go left along Dinas Olau Road. Cross a lane and walk uphill. Follow the lane around to the right to reach a fork. Take the left-hand lane uphill. In about 60 metres turn left on a path to rise above the lane just walked. Ignore any paths leading off it.

3. Go through a gate and ignore gates on the left. In about another 200 metres, the track bears around to the right to have Y Bermo below on the right. In 80 metres, the track bears left uphill. Do not follow it, but continue ahead on a lesser track.

4. Go through a gate and in another 100 metres bear right through a small gate to the semi-circular stone seat on Dinas Olau. Go ahead to reach a path and turn left to descend the hill. Follow it around to the right but, at a junction of paths, bear left to reach another path where there is a gate on the left in the top wall.

5. Go through the gate and follow the right-hand wall. In about 100 metres there is a small gate on the right giving access to the Frenchman's Grave. After visiting the grave, continue beside the wall. Further on, there are fine views of the estuary and viaduct.

6. Pass a seat and ignore a path on the left. Go downhill to a gate in the wall. Do not go through but turn right to have the wall on your left. Pass a bungalow on the left. On reaching a level area where there is a quarry on the right, bear left away from the quarry and descend a path through gorse. Go down a long flight of steps to the A496 and turn left.

7. In approximately 120 metres, cross the road – with care – to a footpath. It descends to run alongside the railway line. Go through the tollgate and follow the bridge across the Afon Mawddach estuary. In clear weather there are magnificent views of the estuary and Cadair Idris range. Porth Penrhyn is only 500 metres to the west.

8. At the end of the bridge, go through a gate and continue ahead to another one. At Morfa Mawddach Station go through a gate on the right to cross the line. Go over a stile and follow the path, which shortly bears left. Walk along the embankment to where it emerges on the road leading to Porth Penrhyn. Either bear right along a footpath for over a kilometre to Porth Penrhyn Station or turn left and follow the narrow gauge line to the station in Fairbourne.

Ffestiniog Railway

The history of the Ffestiniog Railway began in 1798 when William Alexander Madocks bought land around the Afon Glaslyn estuary. His interest in landscape design and town planning led to the construction of the mile-long embankment called Y Cob across the estuary and the new harbour of Port Madoc (now called Porthmadog). Meanwhile, from the 1760s, slate had been worked on a small scale in the mountains around Blaenau Ffestiniog. Pack animals and carts carried the slate to the quays on Afon Dwyryd where it was loaded into small boats and taken downstream to be transferred onto seagoing ships. As new quarries opened, it became obvious that this method of transport limited production.

Plans were put forward for a rail connection to the new harbour and in May 1832 the railway was incorporated by an Act of Parliament. James Spooner was the surveyor of the 1ft 11½inch (597mm) gauge line opened in April 1836. For some years the slate trains descended by gravity and horses (that had ridden down) hauled the empty wagons back up the line. An increase in the production of slate and a demand for passenger services led to the introduction of steam locomotives in 1863. Passenger services started one year later. Traffic increased but, rather than building a double line, larger more powerful locomotives were bought into service. Designed by the ingenious engineer Robert Fairlie, these were double-bogie engines that looked like two locomotives back to back. The *Iarll Meirionnydd (Earl of Merioneth)* was built to this design.

After the 1914-18 war, the slate industry declined and the line became more dependent on tourism. Passenger services stopped at the beginning of the Second World War and the line closed in 1946. Railway enthusiasts formed a group to rescue the railway and by 1958 trains were running as far as Tan-y-bwlch. Problems lay head at Y Dduallt because the British Electricity Authority had installed a power station and submerged the railway line near Tanygrisiau. A new tunnel was built and, to reach it, a spiral was engineered to raise the line. The work was done mainly by volunteers. By 1978, trains ran to Tanygrisiau and in 1983 the station at Blaenau Ffestiniog was officially opened. Trains now run again between Blaenau Ffestiniog and Porthmadog.

Steam locomotives used include *Taliesin*, built 1999; *David Lloyd George*, built 1922; *Iarll Meirionnydd (Earl of Merioneth)* built 1979; *Prince*, built 1864; *Linda* and *Blanche* from the Penrhyn Quarry, both built in 1893.

Trains run every day from the end of March to early November, There are also trains at February half-term, March weekends and some days in November and December, including Boxing Day to New Year's Day.

Walk 8   3½ miles (5.6 kilometres)

Minffordd – Portmeirion – Porthmadog

Route: An easy walk taking in field paths and tracks
                with the option of visiting Portmeirion.
Start: Ffestiniog Railway, Minffordd Station.
Finish: Ffestiniog Railway, Porthmadog Station.
Facilities: Refreshments and toilets at the finish.
Time: 2-2½ hours (more if visiting Portmeirion).
OS Map: 1:25 000 Outdoor Leisure 18.

The Italianate village of Portmeirion may be visited by
following this walk from Minffordd. Clough Williams-Ellis
created this exotic, fascinating place to prove that a beautiful
site could be developed without spoiling it. His dream was to
find a place close to the sea, but off the beaten track, a site that
was rocky, hilly and wooded with some old buildings as a
starting point. He found his requirements on the peninsula that
juts out between the estuaries of Afon Glaslyn and Afon
Dwyryd. Near the water's edge was an old mansion and
buildings to form the nucleus of the village. Some buildings
were built from scratch but many features have been rescued
from demolition elsewhere. Part of the estate is a wild garden
(*Gerddi'r Gwyllt*) covered with trees and shrubs such as
rhododendrons, azalea, palms and eucalyptus. A network of
paths permit exploration. *The Prisoner* was filmed here and a
shop sells mementoes of the television series. Noel Coward
stayed in the village whilst writing *Blithe Spirit*.

Between Portmeirion and Y Cob the walk passes close to
Penrhyn Isa farm where a murder took place in 1812. The
victim was an eighteen years old servant called Mary Jones. She
had been left alone whilst the tenant farmer and his family were
working in the fields. She was stabbed to death whilst money

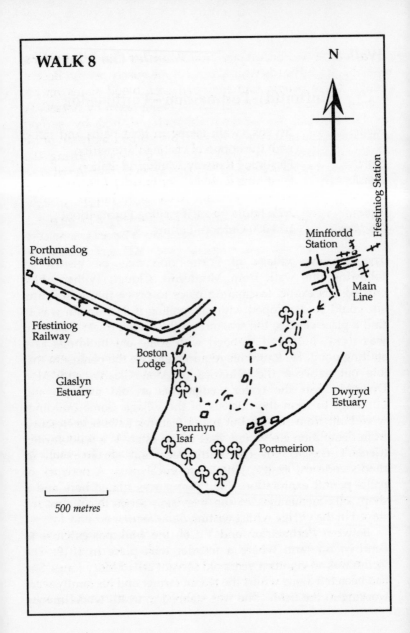

WALK 8

N

Porthmadog
Station

Ffestiniog
Railway

Glaslyn
Estuary

Boston
Lodge

Penrhyn
Isaf

500 metres

Minffordd
Station

Ffestiniog Station

Main
Line

Dwyryd
Estuary

Portmeirion

and a watch had been taken from a dresser. Suspicion fell on one Thomas Edwards who worked at the quarry behind Boston Lodge. Local people said they had seen blood stains on his clothes. He was arrested but, whilst being taken by horseback to Tan-y-bwlch, he escaped although escorted by several constables. The next day he was recaptured but, sadly, an uncle of the murdered young woman was drowned during the search. Thomas Edwards was brought to court on 15 April 1813 in Bala, found guilty and publicly hanged in Dolgellau two days later. The walk passes above Boston Lodge, now workshops of the Ffestiniog Railway but formerly a lodge of the men who built the cob. William Alexander Madocks, who was responsible for its construction, was MP for Boston in Lincolnshire, hence its name.

Walk Directions:

1. From Minffordd Station walk out to the main road (A487) and turn right. Cross the road at the traffic lights and take a road on the left, signposted Portmeirion. In about 40 metres, ignore the road on the right for Portmeirion and continue ahead, soon going downhill.

2. After following the road for about 200 metres, bear right through a gate at a footpath signpost. Follow the left boundary and, at a gate, bear right uphill, beside the fence. To your left are fine views of the Afon Dwyryd estuary.

3. Go through a gate and turn left along a track. In 150 metres, at a bridleway sign, turn right uphill. Cross a road and follow the bridleway, which bends to the left. Go through a gate into a field. Walk beside the right-hand boundary to a gap where there was once a gate and pass a barn on the right.

4. On reaching a track junction, take the first track on the left.

Pass a house on the right and go through the field gate ahead. Follow the right boundary and cross a ladder stile near an old gate in the right corner. The walk bears right here, but to visit Portmeirion turn left to follow the fence to the car park. Walk straight across to the entrance gates. Return the same way to continue the walk.

5. Return to the ladder stile and bear left between fences. The path swings right uphill. Go through a gate and continue uphill beside a right-hand wall and fence. Pass through another gate and walk ahead to a track junction where there is a cattle grid on your right.

6. Turn left along a track and where it bends left at the farm buildings of Penrhyn Isaf, leave it to walk ahead through a field gate. Follow the left boundary of the field and bear right at the corner. Ignore a gate on the left and, after passing the corner fence, continue ahead on a grassy track which descends and bears left to a field gate.

7. Walk ahead and follow the track as it bears right. Below on your left is the Afon Glaslyn estuary. The track descends and passes above Boston Lodge. Go through a gate and follow the main track to a junction. Bear left, downhill, to a stile.

8. Cross the Ffestiniog Railway line and turn left. Before reaching buildings, bear right on a track to the A487. Cross carefully and turn left. Pass the Toll House and, in about another 100 metres, cross the road to some steps going up to a path beside the Ffestiniog Railway line. Follow it across Y Cob to Porthmadog Station.

Walk 9   *4, 5½ or 7 miles (6.5, 9 or 11.5 kilometres)*

Tan-y-bwlch – Rhiw Goch – Penrhyndeudraeth – Minffordd

Route: Forest paths to Rhiw Goch. From Penrhyn there is the option of a short route close to the railway line or a longer walk through unusual scenery.

Start: Ffestiniog Railway, Tan-y-bwlch Station.

Finish: Penrhyn or Minffordd Station.

Facilities: Cafe and toilets at Tan-y-bwlch Station. Camp site near Penrhyndeudraeth.

Time: 3 hours to Penrhyn. If walking on to Minffordd, allow an extra 1 or 2 hours.

OS Map: 1:25 000 Outdoor Leisure 18.

Tan-y-bwlch station opened in July 1873 to bring supplies to the Tan-y-bwlch estate and to take out timber. The influential Oakley family who live on the estate at Plas Tan-y-bwlch owned land and slate quarries at Blaenau Ffestiniog.

On the way to Penrhyn, the walk passes Rhiw Goch, present day passing loop for trains but a horse station during the years 1836-63. At that time, the line was divided into sections with horses being exchanged at the Moelwyn Tunnel, Hafod Llyn and Rhiw Goch. Ten minutes were allowed for the change over before horses rode back to the start of their section in a dandy wagon behind the slate filled gravity train.

The short route from Penrhyn stays close to the railway line whilst the longer route explores unusual, picturesque countryside which was once covered by the sea. The rocky crags were islands at high tide before William Alexander Madocks built his embankment.

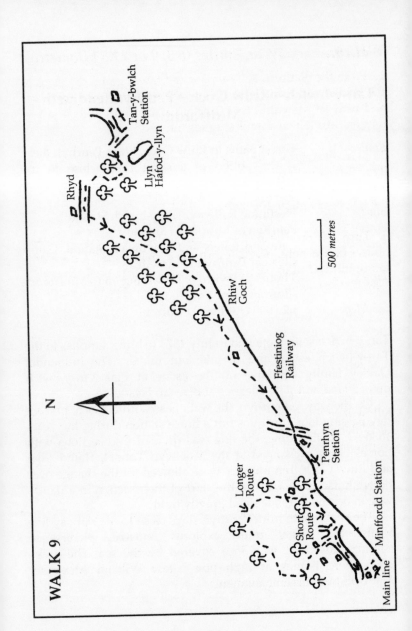

WALK 9

N

Tan-y-bwlch Station

Rhyd

Llyn Hafod-y-llyn

500 metres

Rhiw Goch

Ffestiniog Railway

Penrhyn Station

Longer Route

Short Route

Minffordd Station

Main line

50

Walk Directions:

1. From the platform at Tan-y-bwlch Station go up the steps to the bridge and turn right. Follow the enclosed path to a lane and turn left downhill to a junction. Turn right and, in a few metres, bear left on a track through a forest.

2. Stay on the track until reaching the head of Llyn Hafod-y-llyn. Take a path on the right (post 16) and follow it uphill. In about 200 metres, it starts to descend and, at a gap in a wall on the left, bear right to the lane.

3. Turn left for 500 metres to the village of Rhyd. At some houses on the right, bear left through a kissing-gate. Go slightly left uphill and, after passing through a wall gap, walk downhill. Pass through a broad gate and ignore a small gate on the left.

4. Continue ahead through a long field and cross a stile into the forest. Follow the clear path for about a kilometre to where it emerges on a broad track (post 34). Turn right to a track junction (post 35) and bear left.

5. In approximately 600 metres turn left on a footpath and follow it to a wall beside the Ffestiniog Railway line. The path runs alongside it for about 60 metres then rises a little whilst continuing parallel to the railway. On reaching the railway again, cross a stile.

6. Pass the loop and lights at Rhiw Goch. Shortly, veer slightly to the right, uphill, to a waymarked post. Follow the path ahead. After going through a gap in a wall, bear right to emerge on a track. Turn left through gates and walk along the farm access road to reach a road near a level crossing.

7. Turn left over the crossing and follow the pavement for

about 300 metres. Pass behind the station and, at the end of a wall on the right, turn right on an enclosed path. Go up steps to emerge near Penrhyn Station platform. If continuing to Minffordd, turn left to pass a bakery on your left.

8. Follow the lane downhill to a road junction. Continue ahead and take the first road on the right. In about 50 metres, bear right on a track that veers left past gardens. The Ffestiniog Railway line is above on the right.

9. When the track emerges on a lane, cross directly over to go uphill towards Capel Nasareth. Pass it on your left and follow a path beside the railway line. Ignore a stile to cross it and a stile into a garden. Bear left over a low stile across the path and descend to a lane.

10. Turn right uphill to pass under a bridge and turn left on a track. (If you are following the short route, in about 50 metres, where the track bends right, go ahead on a path beside the railway. Emerge in a field and walk on close to the line. Go through a kissing-gate and bear left on a track past houses to a lane. Turn right and follow the lane around to the left. After passing the second lane on the right, you join the longer route at point 15.)

11. If following the longer route, continue along the track when it bends to the right. Go through coniferous trees and, at a long building, ignore the track on the right. Veer slightly left and walk ahead on a fenced track. Before reaching gates to a house, go left through a small gate into a field. Bear right to pass behind the house and pass through another gate.

12. Walk between trees to a stile then continue ahead through a plantation. On reaching a waymarked post, bear right to a ladder stile. Cross and turn left to have a fence on the left. Walk

uphill, cross a stile and go over a ridge. Descend beside a wall to reach a track.

13. Turn left through a gate and follow the track through woodland to join a track coming from the right. Maintain your direction and, in about 300 metres, bear left to a lane. Turn right for 400 metres and, at a house, veer left on a track.

14. Cross a ladder stile on the left and follow the right-hand fence through a long field. In the far corner, go up steps to a small gate and bear left uphill on a path. Pass through a gate and walk downhill to another. Follow a lane past cottages to a junction and turn right.

15. The two routes join here and follow the lane downhill past houses. Go uphill to pass under pylon cables. On nearing a house on the left, bear left between a building and the house to follow a path. Cross a stile and walk on beside the main line railway to Minffordd Station. Pass the shelter and bear left up the ramp to the Ffestiniog Railway Station.

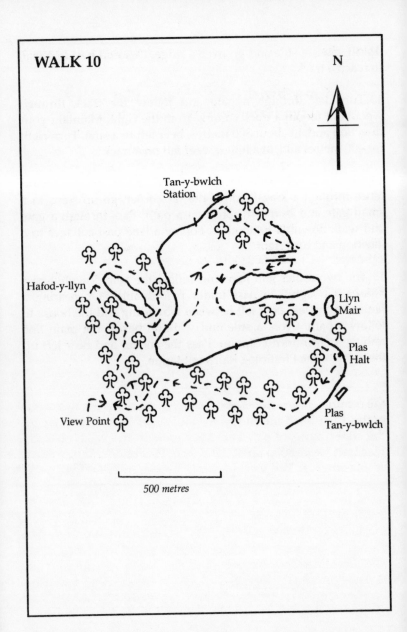

WALK 10

N

Tan-y-bwlch
Station

Hafod-y-llyn

Llyn
Mair

Plas
Halt

Plas
Tan-y-bwlch

View Point

500 metres

Walk 10   5 miles (8 kilometres)

Tan-y-bwlch – Llyn Mair – Plas Halt –
Llyn Hafod-y-llyn – Tan-y-bwlch

Route: Paths and tracks through varied woodland,
                    visiting two lakes and viewpoints of the
                    Ffestiniog Valley.
Start/Finish: Ffestiniog Railway, Tan-y-bwlch Station.
Facilities: Seasonal Cafe and toilets at Tan-y-bwlch
                    Station.
Time: 3½ hours.
OS Map: 1:25 000 Outdoor Leisure 18.

Between Tan-y-bwlch Station and Llyn Mair, the walk follows
the route of the Coed Llyn Mair Nature Trail through the
remains of an ancient oakwood. An informative leaflet is for
sale in the cafe. A wide variety of wild life may be seen on the
nature trail and during the rest of the walk. Jay, woodpecker,
buzzard and pied flycatcher (in summer) are some of the birds
to look out for. On a warm summer's day, butterflies such as
the comma and green-veined white may be fluttering beside the
paths. Llyn Mair and the lower mill pond provided water for
the water powered saw and flour mills in the valley. Beyond
Plas Halt views open up of the Vale of Ffestiniog and the village
of Maentwrog. The embankments beside Afon Dwyryd were
built in the late 18th century to reclaim agricultural land.

Below the railway are the roofs of Plas Tan-y-bwlch,
residential study centre for the Snowdonia National Park and
former home of the Oakley family. In the late 18th century, the
heiress of the Tan-y-bwlch estate, Margaret Griffiths, married
William Oakley from the English Midlands. He enlarged the
house, improved the estate and rebuilt the church at
Maentwrog. A few years after his son inherited the estate, slate

quarries were opened up on Oakley land near Blaenau Ffestiniog and W.G. Oakley laid the first stone for the railway on 26 February 1833. W.G. Oakley's widow built a quarryman's hospital in Blaenau Ffestiniog. The estate remained in the hands of the Oakley family until the last member, Mrs Inge, died in 1961, aged 96.

Walk Directions:

1. From Tan-y-bwlch Station platform, go up the steps to the bridge and descend in the direction of the cafe. Turn left and go through a small gate on the right. Descend the path to a lane.

2. Cross the lane and go through a gate. With Llyn Mair on your left, follow the track. Cross a stile at a gate and, in about another 100 metres, leave the track to take a path on the left. After crossing a stream and going through a gap in a wall, bear left and follow the path beside Llyn Mair. Ignore a track on the right (at post 10) and, a few metres beyond the end of the lake (post 11), turn right on a track.

3. In about 100 metres, at the top of a short rise, go up a few steps on the right and follow a path up the steep hill. Cross a stile and the Ffestiniog Railway line to steps and a stile. Turn left on a path parallel to the line and go through a tall gate. Pass behind Plas Halt platform.

4. Continue along the path to have the railway line on your left. Views open up of Afon Dwyryd and Maentwrog village in the valley below. Pass above Plas Tan-y-bwlch and arrive at a path junction (post 4).

5. Turn right and go through a gap in the wall. Walk ahead on a path through woodland. Further on, it runs alongside a fence. Emerge on a track and continue ahead with the fence on your left.

6. At a track junction, turn right for 200 metres to post 7. Ignore a track and a path on the right and follow the main track. In about 200 metres, leave it to go left on a wide path uphill to a path junction (post 18). The walk turns right here, but if energy and time permit, go on uphill another 300 metres to post 32. Turn left for 60 metres on a level path to a fine viewpoint – take care – on a crag above Llyn Trefor. Views extend to the estuary and Harlech Castle. Return to post 18 and turn left.

7. After a fairly level stretch, the path descends gradually, whilst bearing slightly right. When Llyn Hafod-y-llyn and a track are in view a few metres below, bear left on a narrow path above the track and lake. Go through a gap in a wall and cross a stream. Emerge on a track and turn right a few metres to reach the wide track above the lake.

8. Turn left and, in 150 metres, ignore a path on the left at post 16. Pass around the end of the lake and, in a few metres, bear right on a path to have the lake nearby on your right. The path rises and passes a picnic table then descends through trees before bearing right to pass beside the lake. Cross a stream and walk up to a track.

9. Turn left for a few metres then bear left to follow another track downhill to a ladder stile and gate. Cross the Ffestiniog Railway line to a stile and continue along the track. Ignore a path on the right and turn left at a junction. On rejoining your outward route, retrace your steps to the picnic area at Llyn Mair and Tan-y-bwlch Station.

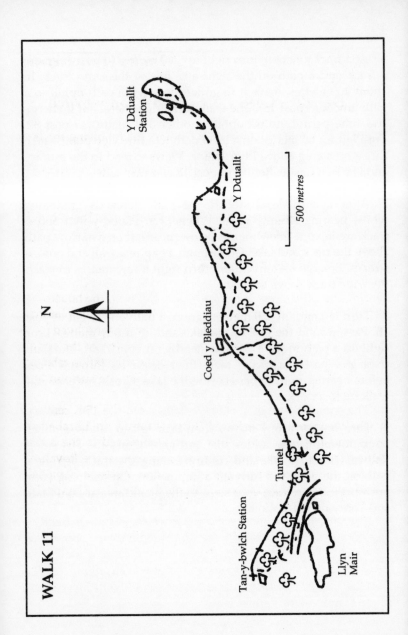

WALK 11

N

500 metres

Y Dduallt Station

Y Dduallt

Coed y Bleddiau

Tunnel

Tan-y-bwlch Station

Llyn Mair

Y Dduallt – Coed y Bleiddiau – Tan-y-bwlch

Route: Woodland and hillside paths following the line
                  of the Ffestiniog Railway.
Start: Ffestiniog Railway, Y Dduallt Station (request
                  stop).
Finish: Tan-y-bwlch Station.
Facilities: Seasonal cafe and toilets at Tan-y-bwlch
                  Station.
Time: 1½-2 hours.
OS Map: 1:25 000 Outdoor Leisure 18.

During the early years of the Ffestiniog Railway, the house at Y
Dduallt station was the station master's house. On the platform
there is a memorial seat to Colonel Campbell who lived at Y
Dduallt Manor and helped with the construction of the spiral.
He was licensed to use explosives. From the orientation table on
the hill above the station are wide views over the surrounding
countryside.

The manor house of Y Dduallt dates from the 15th century.
It was the home of the Lloyd (Llwyd) family in Elizabethan
times and it is said that Oliver Cromwell stayed in the house
during the Civil War whilst campaigning against the Royalists.
In 1962, the manor was bought by Colonel Andrew Campbell
who kept his own locomotive. Above the house is Campbell's
Platform, present day halt for the manor.

Further on, the walk passes a cottage called Coed y
Bleiddiau which was built by the Ffestiniog Railway about 1860
to house a railway inspector. It was rented for a while by the
father of Kim Philby, the Soviet spy. There is a rumour that the
Second World War German propagandist William Joyce (Lord
Haw-Haw) stayed at the cottage.

Walk Directions:

1. At Y Dduallt Station, walk along the platform in the direction of Porthmadog and cross a stile on the right. Bear left and pass under a bridge. Turn right and, in a few paces, go left through trees. Follow a path past crags to a ladder stile. Cross the railway line and bear right, downhill, to Y Dduallt Manor.

2. Follow the access track for a few paces then bear right on a path uphill to have the manor's garden on your right. Go through a gate and cross a stile. Descend to a small bridge over a stream and walk uphill. The path rises and falls a few times before running close to the line and passing the cottage called Coed y Bleiddiau.

3. Descend to cross a footbridge and follow the path to a fork. Take the left-hand path and go through a small gate to enter coniferous woodland. Ignore a path on the left and pass through a gate. Walk downhill to a junction and bear right uphill. Go through a small gate near a cattle grid and turn left to follow the track to a road.

4. Turn right to pass Llyn Mair on your left. A few paces before reaching a gate giving access to a picnic area on your left, cross a footbridge on your right and follow a path uphill to Tan-y-bwlch Station.

Walk 12   5½ miles (9 kilometres)

Y Dduallt – Tanygrisiau Reservoir (Llyn Ystradau) – Afon Goedol – Y Dduallt

Route: Moorland to Tanygrisiau Reservoir followed by forest paths, waterfalls and a steep climb back to Y Dduallt Station.

Start/Finish: Ffestiniog Railway, Y Dduallt Station.

Facilities: None on the route.

Time: 4 hours

OS Map: 1:25 000 Outdoor Leisure 18.

The spiral at Y Dduallt was built because the original line near Tanygrisiau had been submerged by the hydro-electric pumped storage scheme. The deviation from the original track bed raises the line 35 feet, and goes through the new 287 yards tunnel before passing behind the power station to rejoin the old line at Tanygrisiau. The Queen opened the power station in 1963. Water released from Llyn Stwlan, a corrie lake below the Moelwyn mountains, drops 300 metres to drive the generators. During the night, when the demand for electricity is low, water from the reservoir is pumped back to Llyn Stwlan by using electricity from the National Grid.

Near the lake, the walk passes the site of a granite quarry below Moel Ystradau. Worked from about 1919 to the 1930s, it produced macadam for roads. Further on, from the forest track, a house can be seen below, close to Afon Goedol. It is the old Dolwen power station that supplied electricity to nearby quarries and Blaenau Ffestiniog in the early 20th century. After passing Cymerau waterfall, the walk enters Woodland Trust land where many flowers, including wood sorrel and wood avens, are present in spring. The old farmhouse called Cymerau Isaf dates from the 16th century.

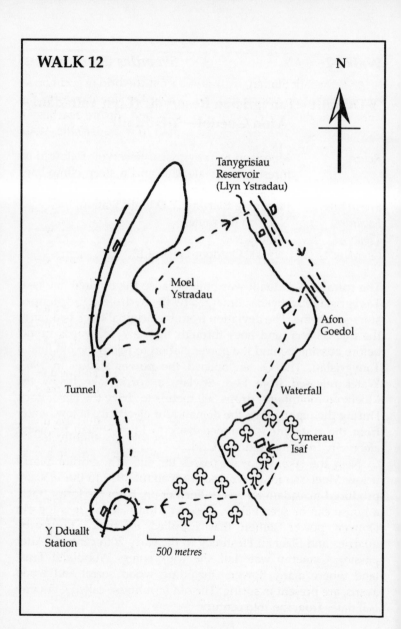

WALK 12

N

Tanygrisiau
Reservoir
(Llyn Ystradau)

Moel
Ystradau

Afon
Goedol

Tunnel

Waterfall

Cymerau
Isaf

Y Dduallt
Station

500 metres

Walk Directions:

1. At Y Dduallt Station, walk away from the bridge and house. Pass a shelter on your right and, where the line curves to the right, cross the line onto the old track bed. Before reaching a fence and gate, veer right down a path to a ladder stile. Walk through the trees to a track.

2. Turn left uphill to the old track bed and bear right along it. Go under an old bridge and, in about another 100 metres, bear left along a track that passes closer to the present line. On your right is the entrance to the old tunnel. Go uphill and ignore another track on the left. Pass through a gate (or over a stile above on the left) and follow the track downhill to have views of Tanygrisiau Reservoir.

3. Ignore a stile on the left next to the railway line. In a few more metres, take a narrow path on the right. It heads in the direction of a quarried hill that has pylons crossing it. In about 400 metres it descends slightly near an inlet of the lake. Go uphill to a level area and pass a ruin on the right. Follow a fence but, in about 50 metres, veer left away from it to reach a track.

4. The track bears right to pass the quarried hill. Pass under cables coming from the power station and go slightly left to have a marshy area on the right. The path rises a little to a fork. Bear right to cross a stile.

5. Follow a path which bears slightly left through bracken and heather. Pass some marshy ground on the right and a stony hill on the left. Descend to a wall and follow it on your left to a footbridge. Walk up to a kissing-gate and road.

6. Turn right along the grass verge. Pass houses on the left and a cottage on the right. In a few more metres, go through a

kissing-gate on the left and slant right uphill over boggy ground and slabs of rock. The path soon improves and runs parallel to the road. Descend gently through bracken to a track near a cattle grid. Bear right through a kissing-gate.

7. Cross the road and turn right. In about 100 metres, turn left along a track. Cross a bridge over Afon Goedol and ignore a descending track on the left. Walk uphill and pass a house on the right.

8. Bear right a few paces then go left onto a path where trees have recently been harvested. Follow a line of painted posts through a felled area of forest. Continue through woodland and another felled area. Take a path through more trees to a path junction. Turn left to a footbridge but, before crossing it, turn left to the waterfalls.

9. Cross the bridge and continue along the path. Where it bears left, go through the small gate ahead onto Woodland Trust land. Walk through deciduous trees to a track junction at a garage. Turn right along a track and follow it into a field. Before reaching a recently restored longhouse, bear left through a gate.

10. Pass a barn on the left and go through a kissing-gate. When the path turns left, bear right to a stile. Go downhill on a narrow path to join a wider path near a wall. Turn right downhill to a stile. Descend to the river and bear right on a path. Cross a footbridge over the river and bear left to have the river on your left.

11. In about 50 metres, the path veers right and climbs steeply away from the river into forest. Cross a stream and continue uphill on a clear path. In a couple of places there are short easy scrambles up rocks. Cross a stile to leave the forest and maintain your direction beside a wall.

Devil's Bridge (*Pontarfynach*) Station (Vale of Rheidol Railway)

Rheidol Falls (Walk 1)

Tywyn Wharf Station (Tal-y-llyn Railway)

Afon Dysynni (Walk 2)

Lower Falls Dôl-goch (Walk 3)

Abergynolwyn (Walk 4)

Nant Gwernol Station (Walks 4 & 5 Tal-y-llyn Railway)

Approaching Penrhyn Point
(Fairbourne & Barmouth Steam Railway)

Goleuwern quarry (Walk 6)

Mawddach estuary (Walk 7)

Porthmadog Station
(Ffestiniog Railway)

Llyn Mair (Walk 10)

Dduallt Station (Walks 11, 12 and 14, Ffestiniog Railway)

The track to Tanygrisiau Reservoir (Walk 12)

Capel Rhosydd, Cwmorthin (Walk 13)

Rhosydd Barracks (Walk 13)

Waunfawr Station (Welsh Highland Railway)

Llanberis Path (Walk 16, Snowdon Mountain Railway)

Great Orme Tramway

Kashmir goats on the Great Orme (Walk 18)

A special event day on the Llangollen Railway.

Llangollen Canal (Walk 19)

Castell Dinas Brân (Walk 19)

Mill site, Nant y Pandy (Walk 21)

Glyndyfrdwy Station (Walks 21 and 22 Llangollen Railway)

Llangollen Railway in the Dee valley, near Carrog.

Carrog (Walk 22)

Bala Station (Bala Lake Railway)

Llyn Tegid (Walk 24)

Llangywer Halt (Walks 24 and 25 Bala Lake Railway)

St Mary's Well, Llanfair Caereinion (Walk 26)

Llanfair Caereinion Station (Welshpool & Llanfair Railway)

12. Cross a stile on the right and bear left along a vague track above the wall. Join another track coming from a gate and bear right along it. At a fork, bear left and, in about another 80 metres, go left on a path to retrace your steps to Y Dduallt Station.

WALK 13

N

Plas
Cwmorthin

Llyn
Cwmorthin

Bwlch
Cwmorthin

Rhosydd
Chapel

Rhosydd

Waterfall

Tanygrisiau
Station

Visitor
Centre

Tanygrisiau
Lake
(Llyn Ystradau)

500 metres

Walk 13   *5½ miles (9 kilometres)*

Tanygrisiau – Llyn Cwmorthin – Rhosydd – Tanygrisiau

Route: This is a linear there and back route so you have the option of turning back at any point. Lanes and tracks ascend to Llyn Cwmorthin and, from the end of the cwm, a track may be followed up to the disused quarry workings at Rhosydd.

Start/Finish: Ffestiniog Railway, Tanygrisiau Station (request stop).

Facilities: Ffestiniog Power Station Visitor Centre. Cafe.

Time: 2-4 hours.

OS Maps: 1:25 000 Outdoor Leisure 17 & 18.

This walk takes you up past a waterfall to the dramatic, enclosed valley of Cwmorthin with its lake and industrial remains. You then have the option of climbing to Bwlch Cwmorthin and the barracks of Rhosydd quarry.

    Cwmorthin quarry, sited on the eastern side of the lake, was first worked in 1810 but was not seriously developed until the 1860s. At its peak five hundred men were employed. Less slate was produced after some of the workings collapsed in the 1880s and later it became part of the Oakley quarry. Quarrymen lived in the houses near the lake and a few metres away stands the remains of their chapel. The ruins of Cwmorthin Uchaf farm lies some distance away on the opposite side of the cwm. It is believed that the same family occupied it for eight hundred years. Before the quarries were developed, Cwmorthin lay on a drovers' route. The track passes the ruins of Rhosydd Chapel, built in 1867, and paid for by the quarrymen. On weekdays it was a school for their children. Further on, to the right of the track, stands the shell of Plas Cwmorthin, built in 1860 for the manager of Rhosydd quarry. Close to the track are the remains of a stable and a terrace of six houses.

The track climbs up to Bwlch Cwmorthin, which was floor nine for the Rhosydd quarry and site of the main mill. The remains of two barracks are still standing and, behind them, the main adit, 600 metres long. Men lodged in the barracks from Monday to Saturday. Higher up the mountain are more barracks and open pits. Worked for about one hundred years, from the 1830s to 1930, Rhosydd was developed into a huge, underground quarry with fourteen levels and one hundred and seventy chambers. About two hundred men were employed. Slate was transported through Cwmorthin by packhorse until C.E. Spooner designed an incline which descends to the Croesor Tramway. Operating from 1864, a tramway ran out to a shelf above Cwm Croesor, from where an incline (less than 1:2 gradient) plunges 200 metres into the cwm.

Walk Directions:

1. From the station walk out to the road and bear right. Pass the Visitor Centre and, at the picnic area, bear right over grass and up steps to join the road again. Turn right to cross the Ffestiniog Railway line and walk uphill. On reaching a bend, ignore the gated road ahead to Llyn Stwlan, and bear right to cross a bridge.

2. On reaching houses, turn left uphill. Pass a parking area and walk up a steep track. Pass a waterfall and, when the track levels out, go through a gate into a 'garden' that has small ponds.

3. Go through another gate and follow a clear path above the river. Ignore a path on the left that climbs up to Wrysgan quarry. Continue along the slate path to ruined houses at Llyn

Cwmorthin. With the lake on your right, take the level track through the cwm. Pass the ruin of Rhosydd Chapel on your left.

4. Before reaching a gate, you will see the ruins of Plas Cwmorthin in trees on your right. Go through the gate across the track and pass the remains of terraced houses on your left. Follow the old track slanting left, uphill. On reaching a level area, notice the large wheelpit on your right. It was never used.

5. Continue uphill to the pass, which was the main working area of Rhosydd quarry. Follow the track ahead for about 800 metres to enjoy magnificent views of Cwm Croesor and Y Cnicht. Retrace your steps to the start at Tanygrisiau Station.

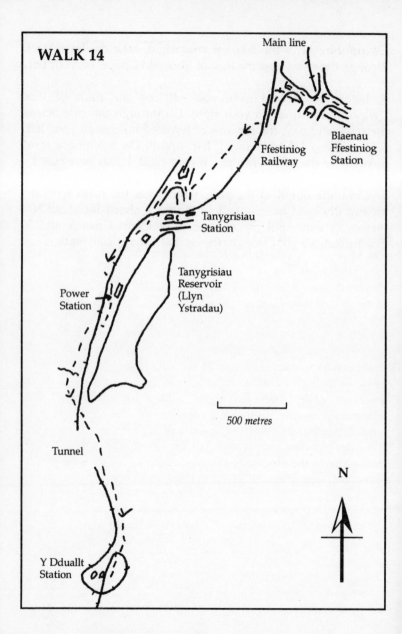

WALK 14

Main line

Blaenau
Ffestiniog
Station

Ffestiniog
Railway

Tanygrisiau
Station

Tanygrisiau
Reservoir
(Llyn
Ystradau)

Power
Station

500 metres

Tunnel

N

Y Dduallt
Station

Walk 14   1¾ or 4 miles (2.7 or 6.5 kilometres)

Blaenau Ffestiniog – Tanygrisiau – Y Dduallt

Route: A moorland walk following the line of the
                  Ffestiniog Railway.
Start: Ffestiniog Railway, Blaenau Ffestiniog Station.
Finish: Tanygrisiau or Y Dduallt Station (request
                  stops).
Facilities: Full facilities in Blaenau Ffestiniog. Cafe at
                  Tanygrisiau.
Time: 1¼ or 3 hours.
OS Map: 1:25 000 Outdoor Leisure 18.

Before the development of the slate industry, Blaenau Ffestiniog
consisted of a few farms and pasture. In the 1760s, Methusalem
Jones of Nantlle came to Ffestiniog after having a dream in
which he discovered slate. He opened a quarry at Diffwys.
Other quarries opened in the early 19th century and, as the
industry developed, a town was hurriedly built for the workers.
Slate was exported all over the world and the settlement soon
became larger than the older village of Ffestiniog, four
kilometres south. Since the decline of the industry, the
population has halved from its peak of 12,000.

After leaving the streets of the town, the route crosses
moorland to the Ffestiniog Railway station near the Tanygrisiau
Reservoir and Visitor Centre. If time, and energy, permit, the
walk can be continued to Y Dduallt Station. In the trees near the
reservoir and power station, is the site of the old farmhouse
called Buarth Melyn which lost its land to the pump storage
scheme. At the far end of the reservoir, the walk follows the old
inclines which were used by the railway in the years 1836-42
before the opening of the 670 metres long old Moelwyn tunnel.
The full slate wagons were hauled up the north incline by the

power of a water wheel and, on the south side, the descending wagons raised the empty ones.

Walk Directions:

1. At Blaenau Ffestiniog Station, go up the steps onto the bridge and walk out to the main road. Turn left and walk downhill to a roundabout and turn left in the direction of Porthmadog. Cross the road and the bridge over the main line and turn right. When the road swings left, continue ahead on a minor road.

2. At a junction, bear left to cross a level crossing over the Ffestiniog Railway line. Pass the King's Head and in another 200 metres, turn right along a track. Cross Afon Barlwyd and a footbridge over the railway line.

3. Enter a garden and bear left uphill to a gate. Continue uphill and pass a small rocky hill on your left. The path descends slightly to a stile and climbs a little to pass above a marshy area, which is on your left. Go through a kissing-gate and walk on to the next one in the left-hand corner. Go downhill to another gate and follow a track to a road.

4. Bear right and, in 50 metres, turn left to cross a bridge. Bear left downhill and cross the railway line. When the road curves left near Tanygrisiau Reservoir, follow it past the Visitor Centre and cafe if you wish to catch the train from Tanygrisiau station. To continue the walk to Y Dduallt, turn right along a road that has a gate across it.

5. Walk uphill and cross the Ffestiniog Railway line again. Continue uphill and, in another 250 metres, bear left along a wide path. Cross a footbridge over a stream, ladder stiles and the railway line. Go downhill between fences behind the hydro-electric power station. At an open area, walk ahead slightly left

towards the reservoir. After crossing a stream, pass trees on the right.

6. At the end of the trees, bear right on a track. In a few paces, swing left on a rough track to arrive at a stile. Recross the Ffestiniog Railway line and bear left on a path above it. Pass remains of the Moelwyn zinc mine mills and bear right to go under the old tramway. Cross a footbridge over a stream and follow the path through a gap in a wall. Cross a stream and descend through bracken to the end of the reservoir and the Ffestiniog Railway line.

7. Cross the line and walk uphill to a track and turn right. After passing through a gate, the track descends and runs parallel to the railway line. On your left is the old tunnel and track bed.

8. Continue along the track to where it joins the old railway track. Turn right and follow it under an old bridge. In about another 100 metres, bear left downhill on a track. After about 80 metres, take a path on the right into a patch of woodland. Follow it to a ladder stile and go up to the old track bed. Cross the new line to the platform at Y Dduallt Station.

Welsh Highland Railway

The original Welsh Highland Railway was formed in 1922 to take over the North Wales Narrow Gauge Railways and the Porthmadog, Beddgelert and South Snowdon Railway. There was already a standard gauge line between Caernarfon and Dinas. The N.W.N.G. Railway operated a line from Dinas Junction to Rhyd-ddu servicing slate quarries. In the year 1875, there had been hopes of building a rack railway from Rhyd-ddu to the top of Yr Wyddfa (Snowdon). The P.B. & S.S. Railway, an amalgamation of smaller companies, had thought the line would be electrified. Part of the route of the Welsh Highland Railway was the horse-drawn Croesor Tramway which carried slate from Cwm Croesor to Porthmadog. The line between Dinas and Rhyd-ddu was reopened for passenger traffic with the locomotive *Russel*. A new track had to be built between Rhyd-ddu and Croesor Junction, from where the old tramway was made suitable for steam operation. In the 1930s the Welsh Highland Railway was leased to the Ffestiniog Railway but, unfortunately, the line was not a success and it closed in 1937.

In 1961 a society was established to reopen the line and three years later it became the Welsh Highland Light Railway. Trains started running between Porthmadog and Pen-y-Mount in 1980 and this short length of line is still operated by the company. Locomotives include the original *Russel*. The Ffestiniog Railway applied to take over the assets of the former Welsh Highland Railway and the company was granted these powers in 1995. By 1997 trains were running from Caernarfon to Dinas and three years later they reached Waunfawr. When the 1ft 11½inch (597mm) line is complete, it will connect with the Ffestiniog Railway at Porthmadog.

Waunfawr – Moel Smytho – Parc Dudley – Waunfawr

Route: A gradual climb on lanes, tracks and moorland
                 paths leads to the summit of Moel Smytho. The
                 descent is through forest and rough pasture.
Start/Finish: Welsh Highland Railway, Waunfawr Station.
Facilities: Pub and campsite near the station. Public toilets
                 in Waunfawr village. Parc Dudley Nature
                 Reserve.
Time: 3 hours.
OS Map: 1:25 000 Outdoor Leisure 17.

Waunfawr grew as a village with the opening of the slate
quarry on Cefn Du, the mountain above it. In the late 19th
century around two hundred men were employed but the
quarry closed in 1928. The hillside of Cefn Du was chosen by
Guglielmo Marconi in 1914 for the site of his transatlantic
transmitter. As well as transmitting signals, it served as a
listening station during the 1914-18 war but closed in 1939.

On a clear day, the walk offers superb views of the coast,
Ynys Môn and nearby mountains. To the south of Moel Smytho
rises the isolated peak of Mynydd Mawr, sometimes described
as Elephant mountain and, nearby across the valley, Moel Eilio
with Yr Wyddfa further away. On the return to Waunfawr, a
diversion can be made to the Parc Dudley nature reserve where
there are picnic tables and a choice of short, circular walks
through ancient woodland. In the village, Tŷ Capel, the
community museum has a monument to John Evans who went
to America in 1792 to search for the 'Welsh Indians' descended
from Madog ab Owain Gwynedd. According to tradition,
Madog sailed to America from Wales in 1170. John Evans found

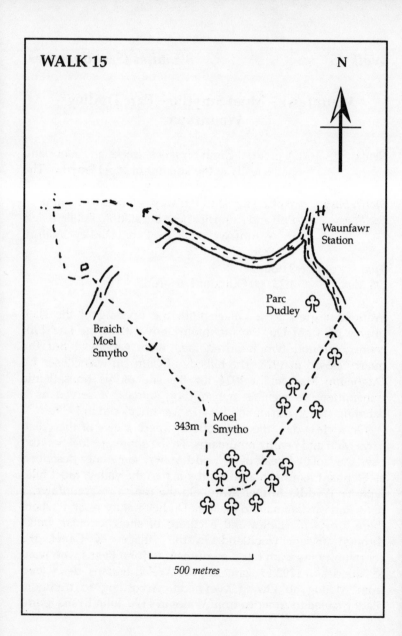

WALK 15

N

Waunfawr
Station

Parc
Dudley

Braich
Moel
Smytho

343m   Moel
Smytho

500 metres

a tribe, the Mandans in Dakota, thought to be the descendants of Madog and his companions but, after staying with them for some months, he came to the conclusion that they were not 'Welsh Indians'. John Evans was the first cartographer to map parts of the northern reaches of the Missouri river.

Walk Directions:

1. From the station, walk out to the car park. On reaching the road, turn left and, in a few metres, bear right on a lane signposted Rhostryfan. Follow the lane uphill for about a kilometre and, where it bends left, leave it to continue ahead on a narrow lane.

2. In about 300 metres, go through a gate across the lane and walk ahead on a rough track between broken walls. Stay on the main track and ignore a track on the right to a house. At a fork, ignore the track on the right that has a cattle grid, but go left through a gate onto an enclosed track. In about another 100 metres, at a point where there is a track on the right and a cattle grid, bear left through a field gate.

3. Walk uphill following a line of trees. On reaching a wall, continue uphill, aiming for the right-hand corner of the field. Walk between walls to a kissing-gate near a broad gate. Go on uphill through open land dotted with gorse. When in line with a wall corner on your left, bear left to a track coming from a farm. Turn right to join a lane.

4. Bear right on the lane and, in about 60 metres, leave it to follow a track on the left. It runs beside a wall. In 400 metres, at a fork, take the right-hand track in the direction of a walled enclosure. On reaching it, follow the right-hand wall to a corner. Leave the wall to walk ahead on a path and ignore a left fork. Ascend the path to the summit of Moel Smytho (343m).

5. Walk ahead, downhill, on a clear path that veers left towards a forest. On reaching a wall, follow it for about 100 metres to a ladder stile on the left. Cross a grassy area and take a path into the forest. Follow the yellow arrow waymarks through the forest. The path crosses a track and continues ahead through a wall gap to a path junction.

6. Turn left to an area where forest has recently been felled on the left-hand side of the path. Follow the path beside the forest to meet a track. At a corner of the forest, where the main track bends right downhill, leave it to go ahead on a stony track.

7. In a few metres, you should reach a post with a yellow arrow. Pass a section of wall and take a footpath slanting right. It passes above ruins. Go through a broken wall and walk downhill following waymarked posts. As you near more forest, the posts may be smaller and lower. Go through another wall and pass a ruin.

8. The path enters the forest and, beyond a fallen tree, the way becomes clearer. Descend to a stile in a wall and walk ahead to pass a waymarked post. Go gradually downhill into trees and cross a broken wall.

9. Bear left and cross a rocky knoll. Pass through a broken wall and climb a ladder stile. Go downhill gradually to a stile in a right-hand wall. Bear left through a narrow field and, where the right-hand wall bends right, leave it to walk ahead to the next stile.

10. Veer right downhill to a kissing-gate and the A4085. Turn left and, in about 250 metres, you will pass Parc Dudley nature reserve on your left. Continue along the road for another 200 metres to Waunfawr Railway Station.

Trên Bach yr Wyddfa –
Snowdon Mountain Railway

The Snowdon Mountain Railway opened on Easter Monday 1896, but had to close on the same day because of an accident. Whilst the locomotive *Ladas* was descending, it left the track and plunged over a precipice. The footplate crew jumped to safety but a passenger suffered fatal injuries after leaping out of his carriage whilst it was in motion. All the other passengers were safe – the locomotive was not coupled to the coaches and these were soon stopped by their own automatic brakes. The line was closed for a year and fitted with guard rails.

Built as a tourist attraction, the rack and pinion railway's gauge is 2ft 7½inch (800mm). There are no level sections and the steepest gradient is 1:5.5. It is a single track with several passing places. The steam locomotives were built at Winterthur in Switzerland. *Ladas*, the ill-fated No. 1, was named after Mrs Laura Alice Duff Assheton Smith, the wife of landowner G.W. Duff Assheton Smith on whose land the railway was constructed. No. 2, *Enid*, was named after the daughter of the landowner. There are five steam locomotives in operation now and several diesels. Carriages are always uphill of the locomotive and, as in 1896, are not coupled to it. The length of time it takes for the train to climb over 3000ft to the summit station is about one hour.

Weather permitting, trains normally operate from mid-March until the first of November. At the beginning of the season and after mid-October they may not go all the way to the summit. Bad weather at any time, such as strong winds, can prevent trains from running. When the weather is fine, especially in July and August, tickets for the trains are sold out very quickly and it is advisable to arrive at Llanberis booking office as early as possible. Trains do not operate to a firm timetable but normally the first train leaves Llanberis at 9.00 am and the service usually continues until mid or late afternoon according to demand. Both return and single tickets are available.

Walk 16   5 miles (8 kilometres)

Pen yr Wyddfa (Snowdon Summit) – Bwlch Glas – Halfway House – Llanberis

Route: A downhill walk following a clear path which runs close to the mountain railway line part of the way. Some sections of path are rough underfoot and steep.

Start: Snowdon Mountain Railway Summit Station.

Finish: Llanberis.

Facilities: Cafe, gift shop, and toilets at the summit. Full facilities in Llanberis.

Time: 2½-3 hours.

OS Map: 1:25 000 Outdoor Leisure 17.

At 1085m (3560ft) Yr Wyddfa is the highest mountain south of the Scottish Highlands. On a clear day there is a magnificent panoramic view over Eryri (Snowdonia) taking in the nearby ridges of Grib Goch and Y Lliwedd, and extending to the Glyder, Carnedd, Moelwyn and Hebog ranges. On exceptionally clear days, which occur only a few times each year, the view stretches to the Lake District of England, Isle of Man and the Wicklow mountains in Ireland. The first recorded ascent was by a botanist, Thomas Johnson, in 1639. By the time George Borrow walked up the path in 1854, many people were ascending or descending the same path.

Yr Wyddfa means 'the burial place' which may refer to Rhita, a mythological giant said to have been killed by King Arthur. Between Yr Wyddfa and Y Lliwedd is Bwlch y Saethau, one of the legendary places where Arthur fought his last battle with Mordred. His knights sleep in a cave on Y Lliwedd precipice waiting for his return. In Cwm Dyli's higher lake, Llyn Glaslyn, lives Yr Afanc, an enormous monster that lived in

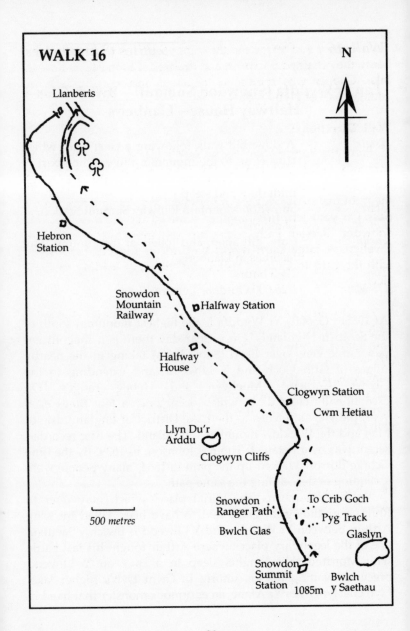

WALK 16

N

Llanberis

Hebron
Station

Snowdon
Mountain
Railway

Halfway Station

Halfway
House

Clogwyn Station

Cwm Hetiau

Llyn Du'r
Arddu

Clogwyn Cliffs

500 metres

Snowdon
Ranger Path

To Crib Goch

Pyg Track

Bwlch Glas

Glaslyn

Snowdon
Summit
Station

1085m

Bwlch
y Saethau

Afon Conwy and terrorised the local people. After catching the beast, they chained it to oxen and dragged it to this high remote lake. Copper was mined in the cwm and miners lived in cottages east of Llyn Llydaw.

Walk Directions:

1. From the Summit Station on Yr Wyddfa, take the path that descends beside the railway. In about 600 metres, you will reach Bwlch Glas, conjunction of several paths. A tall stone on the right marks the zigzags of the Pyg Track rising from Pen-y-pass. On your left, from another stone by the railway line, the Snowdon Ranger Path comes up the mountain from Llyn Cwellyn. A large cairn marks the fork of the Llanberis Path with the path to Crib y Ddysgl and the ridge leading to Grib Goch.

2. Be sure to take the left-hand fork and continue downhill with the railway line a little further distant on your left. The path and line run closely parallel again for a short distance above Cwm Hetiau (Valley of Hats, so named because of the numerous train passengers' hats blown into the cwm). From this point are fine views of the Llanberis Pass and the Glyder Range. Clogwyn Station lies ahead but, 100 metres before it, the path bears left under the railway track.

3. The path is steep for a while but soon eases. A grassy path on the left is an old miners' track, now used by climbers visiting the cliffs of Clogwyn Du'r Arddu. In less than another kilometre you will pass Halfway House.

4. The line is now only a short distance above on your right and in a few hundred metres you will pass below Halfway Station. Soon, the path passes under a railway bridge and runs parallel with the railway line, which is now on your left.

5. The path descends gently and in just over a kilometre passes above Hebron Station. In about another 200 metres go through a small gate and join a lane. Turn right and follow the lane to the A4086, where it emerges opposite the Victoria Hotel. Turn left past the Snowdon Railway Station into Llanberis.

Great Orme Tramway

Having the distinction of being the only cable hauled tramway in Britain, the Great Orme Tramway attracts the interest of railway enthusiasts and tourists alike.

Under the Act of Parliament in 1898, a group of businessmen set up the Great Orme Tramway Company and started building the first section of the line in 1901. Progress was slow and a team of horses was brought in to haul the cables up to Halfway Station. Services began along the lower section on 31 July 1902 and were a great success with seventy thousand passengers being carried by October that year. Services to the summit began in July, 1903. The tramway prospered but in 1932 an accident occurred when the brakes of a tram-car failed and it left the rails. The driver and a young girl were killed and ten passengers were seriously injured. The tramway closed and the company went into liquidation. In 1934, a new company called the Great Orme Railway Ltd took it over and ran the tramway until it was purchased by the local council in 1948. Another accident took place in the year 2000 when two trams collided and over twenty people were slightly injured. The tramway was closed for about fourteen months whilst undergoing improvements.

The mile (1.6 km) long tramway is divided into two sections with a changeover at Halfway Station. The haulage cable for the lower section passes through an underground conduit whilst the cable of the upper section passes over pulleys attached to the sleepers. Coke was used to operate the winding gear until 1956 when a change was made to electricity. A new Halfway Station with a Swiss made tracking system and display of the tramway's history was opened in 2001. The four original tram-cars built in 1902-3 are still in use and there are passing loops on each section.

Trams operate daily Easter to the end of October from 10.00 am to 6.00 pm. Single, return and family tickets are available.

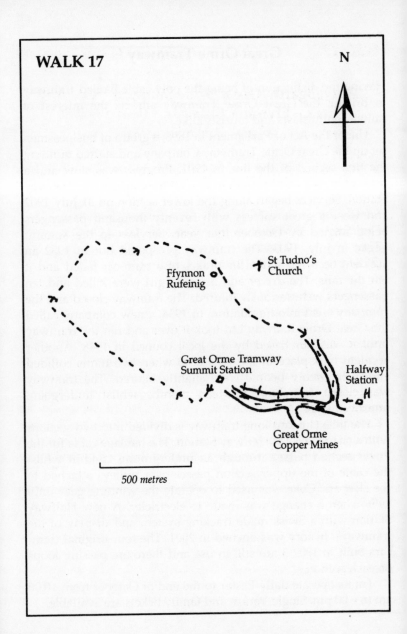

WALK 17

N

St Tudno's Church

Ffynnon Rufeinig

Great Orme Tramway Summit Station

Halfway Station

Great Orme Copper Mines

500 metres

Penygogarth (Great Orme Summit) – Country Park – Ffynnon Rufeinig – Penygogarth (Great Orme Summit)

Route: A walk around the summit of Y Gogarth (the Great Orme) with a fairly easy climb back to the start.

Start/Finish: Great Orme Tramway Summit Station.

Facilities: Visitor centre, toilets, cafe. Great Orme mines.

Time: 2 hours.

OS Map: 1:25 000 Outdoor Leisure 17.

Situated north-east of Llandudno, the Great Orme is a massive limestone headland 679 feet (200m) high. The rocks were formed from sea creatures that lived during the Carboniferous period, an era when much of Wales was covered by shallow sea. Now managed as a country park and nature reserve, the Great Orme is known for its wide variety of wild flowers and butterflies. Birds to look out for in summer include wheatear, meadow pipit and stonechat. You are also likely to see the Kashmir goats that have roamed on the Orme for the last hundred years. The walk passes close to an area of limestone pavements and large rocks (erratics) that were left behind in the Ice Age.

The well passed on the walk, Ffynnon Rufeinig (the Roman Well), is just one of several wells and springs on the Great Orme. There is no evidence to suggest it was used by the Romans. Further on, the route passes above St Tudno's Church. In the 6th century, Tudno, an early Welsh missionary, came to the Great Orme and built a wooden church. It was rebuilt in stone during the 12th century and enlarged three hundred years later. A gale in 1839 tore off the roof, which was not replaced until 1855. Outdoor services are held here during the summer months. Slightly off-route, the Copper Mine complex is well worth a visit. There is evidence that the mines were first worked during the Bronze Age about three and a half thousand years ago.

Walk Directions:

1. From the Summit Station go out to the road and walk downhill towards the sea. Follow a wall on your right and, at a corner, bear right to continue on a path parallel to the wall. Ignore a descending path on the left.

2. Pass a pile of stones at a corner and continue alongside the wall. Further on, on your left, are oddly shaped limestone rocks. On reaching a gate, walk around it and continue along a track. In about 200 metres you will see the well named Ffynnon Rufeinig on your right. Soon, St Tudno's Church is in view below on your left.

3. On reaching a road, turn right and follow it to a junction. Bear right uphill and pass, on the left, a road to the Great Orme Mines. Continue uphill alongside the road to the Summit Station.

Penygogarth (Great Orme Summit) –
Monk's Path – Llandudno

Route:	Descending and level paths comprise the main part of the walk. The short option passes through Haulfre Gardens whilst the longer route climbs to cross the lower slopes of the Orme then descends through Happy Valley.
Start:	Great Orme Tramway Summit Station.
Finish:	Llandudno town centre.
Facilities:	Cafe, toilets and Visitor's Centre at the start. Refreshments in Haulfre Gardens and Happy Valley.
Time:	1½ or 2½ hours.
OS Map:	1:25 000 Outdoor Leisure 17.

The Welsh name Y Gogarth comes from the mists of time, whilst the English 'the Great Orme' is derived from the Viking words *Horma Heva* meaning a serpent. It resembles this shape from the sea. Man has lived on the headland since the Stone Age.

The summit buildings have an interesting history. A telegraph station built here in 1840 was one of a chain that transmitted signals between Caergybi (Holyhead) and Liverpool. Around 1903 the building was enlarged and converted into a hotel with an eighteen-hole golf course nearby. During the Second World War the RAF used it as a radar station but, in 1952, the building was bought by Randolph Turpin, the middle-weight boxing champion. Today, at the complex, there is a cafe and gift shops.

The path to the Marine Drive is known as Ffordd Las because it is always green. It is also known as the Monk's Path

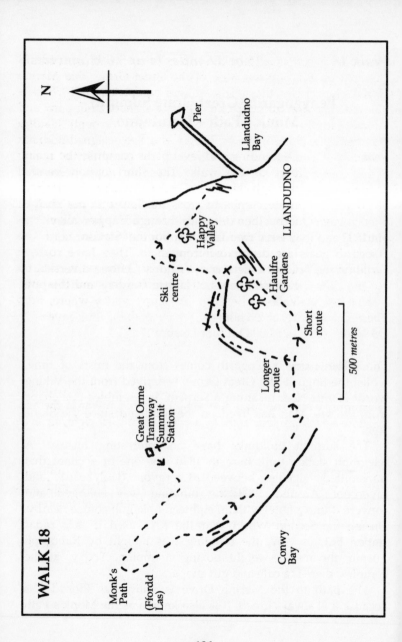

WALK 18

N

Pier

Llandudno Bay

Happy Valley

Ski centre

Great Orme
Tramway
Summit
Station

Monk's Path

(Ffordd
Las)

Conwy Bay

Haulfre Gardens

Longer route

Short route

LLANDUDNO

500 metres

because it connected the Bishop's Palace with St Tudno's Church on the opposite side of the Great Orme. The Marine Drive that circles the headland was completed in 1878 as a tourist attraction for people to enjoy the scenery from pony and horse carriages. The shorter walk returns through Haulfre Gardens, the work of Henry Pochin who also designed Bodnant Gardens. On the longer walk there is the possibility of seeing feral goats. These are the shaggy, Kashmir goats descended from a pair of the Windsor Royal Herd that were given to Sir Mostyn for breeding at Gloddaeth. It is said that the Shah of Persia gave Queen Victoria a couple of goats at her coronation in 1837 and they were the foundation for the Windsor herd. The Gogarth goats are descended from them. They have roamed wild on the headland for about a century. After a diversion on to the cliffs for superb views of Llandudno Bay and the Little Orme, the walk descends through Happy Valley where, from Victorian times to the 1970s, a series of small theatres gave open air performances.

Walk Directions:

1. After exploring the summit, cross the tram line near the terminus. Cross the road and walk downhill towards the sea. Follow a wall on your right to a corner and turn right, to have the sea on your left.

2. In 500 metres, at a waymarked post, turn left to follow a grassy path downhill. Emerge on the Marine Drive and turn left. In 180 metres bear left on a surfaced track. On reaching a fork in about 300 metres, bear right downhill.

3. Pass a house and continue beside a right-hand wall and fence. Go up steps and follow the path below rocks. Emerge on a tarmac path and turn left. It zigzags up to a higher level to give fine views over Llandudno.

4. Walk on for about 300 metres to a path with steps on the left. The path is on the far side of a shelter where there is a seat and small hill on the right. (If following the short walk, continue along the path into Haulfre Gardens. Pass the tea rooms and, at a lane junction, bear right down Tyn-y-maes. Turn left to the Tramway station and town centre.)

5. If following the longer walk, walk uphill and follow a path that bears right on top of the hill. Go through a kissing-gate and walk downhill along a road. Ignore a road on the right. Further on, at a fork, bear right to pass a small green on your left.

6. At a road junction, bear right downhill to have the tramline on your left. In 200 metres, turn left along a lane and pass a car park and The Alpine Lodge Restaurant on your right. Take a right-hand track and path to pass the ski slope and toboggan run. After passing through a kissing-gate, walk on to a path junction and turn right. For views over Llandudno, in a few paces, go left uphill for a short distance.

7. Walk downhill on a path and go through a gate. Descend a zigzag path through Happy Valley Gardens. Pass buildings on the right and follow a road to Marine Drive. Turn right to the pier, promenade and town centre.

Llangollen Railway

The eight mile long Llangollen Railway forms part of a line that originally ran from Rhiwabon to the Cambrian Coast. The Vale of Llangollen Railway from Rhiwabon to Llangollen opened in 1861. Four years later the railway reached Corwen and the whole line was open by 1869. It became part of the Great Western Railway. The journey from Rhiwabon to Y Bermo was fifty-four miles and with thirty-one passenger stops took three hours. The line was also used for freight, especially slate. Increasing car ownership and road haulage, from the mid-20th century onwards, led to a decline in use and lack of profits. The Beeching Report recommended its closure. Most of the line closed a few months prematurely in 1965 because of flooding. However, the Rhiwabon to Llangollen section continued to operate until 1968, after which the track was lifted.

In the early 1970s, the Fflint and Deeside Railway Preservation Society (now called the Llangollen Railway Society) was formed and, in June 1975, work was started on restoring the stations and line. The first passenger trains ran in 1981. The line was opened in sections and trains reached Berwyn in 1985, Glyndyfrdwy in 1992 and Carrog in 1996. There are plans to extend the line to Corwen. This is a standard gauge line and most locomotives are ex G.W.R. and B.R.

Trains operate most days from April to the end of October, February half-term, some February and March weekends and Boxing Day to 1 January.

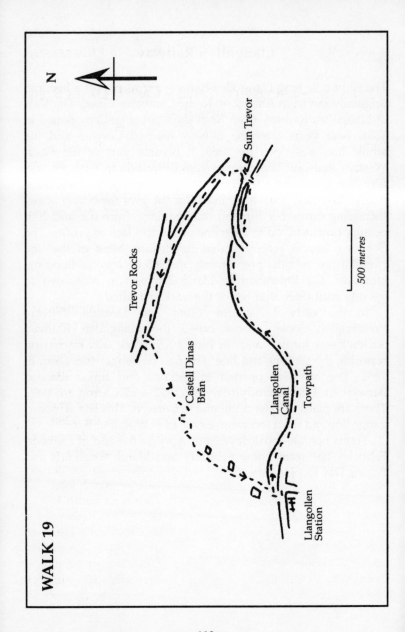

WALK 19

N

Sun Trevor

Trevor Rocks

500 metres

Castell Dinas
Brân

Llangollen Canal

Towpath

Llangollen
Station

110

Walk 19   *5 miles (8 kilometres)*

Llangollen – Llangollen Canal – Castell Dinas Brân – Llangollen

Route:	A stretch of canal towpath is followed by a gradual climb along lanes and paths to the summit of Castell Dinas Brân.
Start/Finish:	Llangollen Railway, Llangollen Station.
Facilities:	Tea room and toilets at the start, pub on the route. Campsites in the area.
Time:	3-3½ hours.
OS Maps:	1:50 000 Landranger 117;
1:25 000 Explorer 255.

Llangollen is known throughout the world for its International Musical Eisteddfod which takes place every July in the pavilion. The famous Ladies of Llangollen lived at Plas Newydd on the south side of the town in the 18th century. Their guests included Wordsworth, Sir Walter Scott and the Duke of Wellington. The walk leaves the town by following the Llangollen canal eastwards for 3 km and then makes a gradual climb to the ruins of Castell Dinas Brân. Built in the 1260s by the lords of Powys, the fortress was in use for only a few years. When Edward I's army arrived in 1277 they found the castle had been deserted and burnt down. An English garrison was stationed there but, later, it was returned to the Welsh lords. In 1282, after Llywelyn ap Gruffudd was killed near Builth Wells, Edward I granted the area to John de Warenne. Rather than repair Castell Dinas Brân, he built a new castle at Holt. The ruin stands on the site of an Iron Age hill fort, said to have been founded by Brân. According to legend, this is one of the places where King Arthur placed the Holy Grail. Another story tells of a golden harp hidden under the castle, waiting to be discovered by a boy and silver-eyed white dog. The hill offers spectacular views of the Eglwyseg escarpment and Vale of Llangollen.

Walk Directions:

1. From Llangollen Station walk out to Abbey Road (the A542). Cross to the opposite pavement and turn left. In a few metres, turn right on a path uphill to the canal.

2. On reaching Llangollen Wharf, turn right on the towpath to go under a bridge. With the canal on your left, continue past moorings and under two more bridges (no. 43 and no. 42). At the next bridge, approximately 3 km from Llangollen wharf, go through a kissing-gate and cross the bridge.

3. Cross the road (the A539) and with the Sun Trefor pub on your right, walk up a lane. Behind the pub, turn left on a drive for Haulfryn. In a few paces, leave it to go up a flight of steps and follow a footpath. Turn left at a path junction.

4. Emerge on a track and bear right to a lane. Turn left and ignore another lane on the right. Ignore a track on the left and follow the lane to a junction.

5. Turn left and pass below Trefor Rocks. Ignore a footpath on the left but, in another 150 metres, turn left on a lane that has a cattle grid. In about 50 metres, go through a kissing-gate on the right and bear left. Follow the waymarks uphill and cross a stile. Go through a gap in an embankment and cross the ditch to make the final climb to Castell Dinas Brân ruins.

6. Walk straight across the hill and descend a path in the direction of Llangollen. At the last zigzag, head towards a house. Go through a kissing-gate and follow a track downhill to a junction.

7. Cross to another track and follow it to a kissing-gate on the right. Continue downhill beside the left-hand fence. Descend a railed path and cross a drive to a kissing-gate. Follow an enclosed path past a school. Cross a road to a bridge over the canal and retrace your steps to the start of the walk.

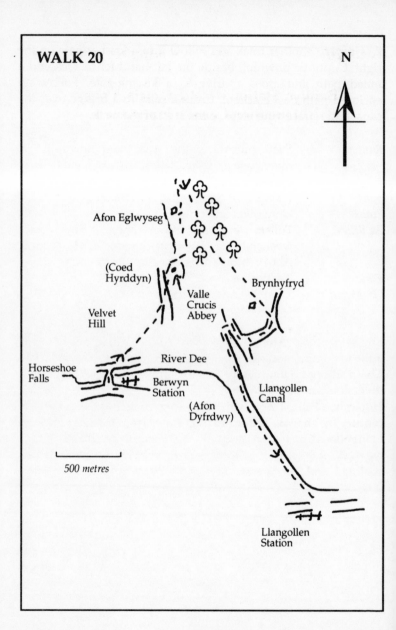

WALK 20

N

Afon Eglwyseg

(Coed Hyrddyn)

Velvet Hill

Valle Crucis Abbey

Brynhyfryd

Horseshoe Falls

River Dee

Berwyn Station

(Afon Dyfrdwy)

Llangollen Canal

500 metres

Llangollen Station

Berwyn Station – Valle Crucis Abbey – Llangollen Canal – Llangollen

Route:	Easy hillside paths, lane and towpath. A diversion can be made to the Horseshoe Falls at the beginning of the walk.
Start:	Llangollen Railway, Berwyn Station.
Finish:	Llangollen Station.
Facilities:	Toilets and tea room open high season weekends at Berwyn Station. Valle Crucis Abbey. Motor museum slightly off-route.
Time:	2½-3 hours.
OS Maps:	1:50 000 Landranger 125 and 117; 1:25 000 Explorer 255.

The bridge over Afon Dyfrdwy (the River Dee) at Berwyn was built to commemorate Edward VII's coronation. Nearby is the Chain Bridge Hotel and its famous suspension bridge. A diversion can be made on the far side of King's Bridge to the Horseshoe Falls, a weir which was constructed in the early 19th century by Thomas Telford to feed water from the river into the Llangollen Canal. An arm of the Shropshire Union Canal network, it was built to form a link between the north Wales coalfield and the Severn, Dee and Mersey rivers. Slate from quarries at the Horseshoe Pass was transported along it, as well as limestone, coal and agricultural products. Trade declined gradually at the beginning of the 20th century with the increasing use of rail and road transport. Pleasure boat trips have operated on the canal since 1884. During the summer months, you are likely to meet horse-drawn barges on your walk along the towpath to Llangollen.

After crossing the National Trust owned land called Coed

Hyrddyn (Velvet Hill), the walk reaches Abaty Glyn-y-groes (Valle Crucis Abbey), a Cistercian abbey founded in 1201 by Madog ap Gruffudd, the Prince of Powys. The best-preserved feature is the chapter house and dormitory above it. Behind the church is the only surviving monastic fishpond in Wales. Opening times are 10.00 am – 5.00 pm. May – September. Now owned by Cadw, the abbey was dissolved in 1537. The name of the Abbey is derived from Eliseg's Pillar, which stands a few hundred metres to the north. Now only half its original size, the cross probably dates from the 9th century and may have been erected by Cyngen in memory of his great-grandfather Eliseg. The weathered inscriptions celebrate the names and victories of the ruling house of Powys.

Walk Directions:

1. From Berwyn Station, walk up to the road and turn right. In a few metres, bear right along the B5103 and follow it under the railway line. Cross the bridge that spans Afon Dyfrdwy (the River Dee) and walk uphill. (To visit the Horseshoe Falls, look for steps on the right that descend to a bridge crossing the canal. Bear right along the towpath to a field and view of the falls.)

2. On reaching a junction, ignore the road on the left but, a few metres further on, take a narrow lane on the left. Immediately, leave it by bearing right on a path signposted Velvet Hill and Valle Crucis Abbey. Go up steps, through trees and cross a stile.

3. Turn right on a footpath along the side of Coed Hyrddyn (Velvet Hill). Pass trees and continue beside a fence to a footpath signpost. Follow the path downhill to a stile.

4. On reaching the road turn left and, in about 50 metres, go through a kissing-gate on the right. Cross the field to another

gate. Turn left to pass Valle Crucis Abbey on your right.

5. At a left bend in the lane, bear right on a track through a caravan site. When the track bends left, go ahead between caravans and cross a footbridge over Afon Eglwyseg.

6. Follow a path that bears slightly right up the hillside, then turn left to a stile beside a gate. Walk along the left side of a long field to a ladder stile near a house. Immediately, turn right to another stile and bear left along a track.

7. In 200 metres turn right on another track, which is signposted Brynhyfryd. Cross two stiles and follow a fence downhill to pass a house on the right. Continue along a track between fields to a lane and turn right.

8. At a junction, in about 100 metres, turn right downhill to emerge on the A542. Bear right downhill and, in approximately 150 metres, turn left on a road going to the Motor Museum.

9. After crossing the bridge over the Llangollen Canal, turn left along the towpath. On reaching the buildings at Llangollen Wharf, descend a path to Abbey Road and Llangollen Railway Station.

WALK 21

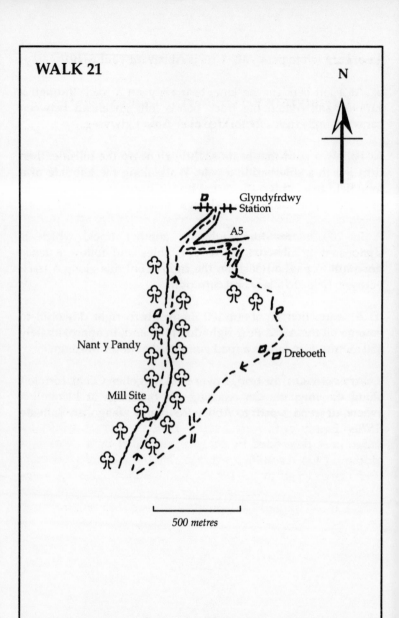

N

Glyndyfrdwy
Station

A5

Nant y Pandy

Mill Site

Dreboeth

500 metres

Walk 21   *2¾ miles (4.5 kilometres)*

Glyndyfrdwy – Dreboeth – Nant y Pandy – Glyndyfrdwy

Route: A gentle climb through fields is followed by an interesting descent along an old tramway and through a wooded gorge.

Start/Finish: Llangollen Railway, Glyndyfrdwy Station.

Facilities: Tea room and toilets open at the start in high season.

Time: 2 hours.

OS Maps: 1:50 000 Landranger 125
                  1:25 000 Explorer 255.

This short, interesting walk descends the fascinating, wooded valley of Nant y Pandy along an old tramway which connected the Deeside and Moel Fferna quarries with Glyndyfrdwy station. Opened in the mid-19th century, the nearer, Deeside quarry connected to a water powered mill at Nant y Pandy by a 2ft 6inch gauge wooden railed tramway. A steel tramway was extended to the underground workings of Moel Fferna in the 1870s. Empty carts were hauled uphill by horses, whilst the laden ones descended by gravity, controlled by a quarryman riding on top controlling a brake. The remains of workshops and a large wheel-pit are passed on the walk. Higher up, near a slab bridge, a reservoir channelled water to power the water-wheel. Deeside quarry, which produced slate for billiard tables, etc., closed in the 1920s whilst Moel Fferna quarry continued to produce roofing slate until 1960. During the last years of its operation, slate was transported by road.

Walk Directions:

1. From Glyndyfrdwy station, walk out to the lane and turn right. Walk uphill to the A5 and turn left along the pavement. Immediately after passing the church, turn right to pass the churchyard gates on your right. Follow the lane around left and right bends, then cross a stile on your left.

2. Climb over another stile and slant slightly to the left as you walk up the field to the next stile. Cross to a stile at the edge of trees. Turn left to another and bear right. Follow a left hand fence but, in a few metres, bear right across the field to a stile.

3. Pass a house on the left and follow a track past buildings to emerge on a lane. Turn right, uphill, in the direction of Dreboeth. Cross a stile at a cattle grid and walk between buildings. Veer left but do not take the path that enters a field. Take a right-hand path through a kissing-gate, passing a building on your right.

4. Walk uphill on a green track and go through a gate. Follow a fence on the left but, when it bends left, continue ahead to another fence. Walk downhill with the fence on your right. Go through a gate and emerge on a lane.

5. Cross the lane to a track and walk downhill. In about 300 metres, at a footpath signpost for Glyndyfrdwy and Nant y Pandy Tramway, bear right on a path. Cross a stile and, shortly, slabs forming a bridge over a stream.

6. Continue downhill through attractive woodland and pass a waterfall. After going through a clearing at the mill site, walk on to a footpath signpost. Go straight ahead, with the stream on your right.

7. On reaching a cottage, cross a footbridge and bear left along a track. Pass a house on the right and walk ahead to emerge on the A5. Cross the road carefully and turn right. In a few metres, turn left and retrace your steps to Glyndyfrdwy station.

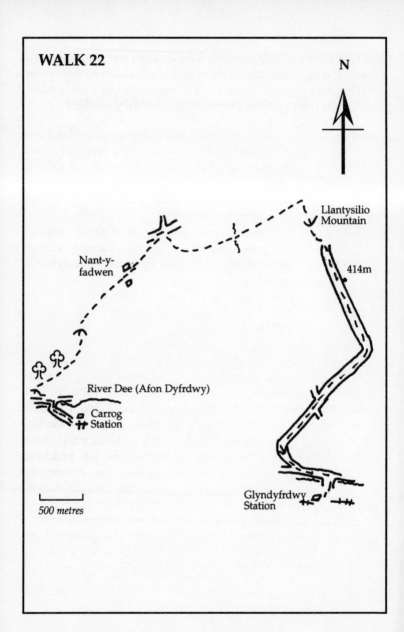

WALK 22

N

Llantysilio
Mountain

414m

Nant-y-
fadwen

River Dee (Afon Dyfrdwy)

Carrog
Station

500 metres

Glyndyfrdwy
Station

Walk 22   *6½ miles (10.5 kilometres)*

Carrog – Nant-y-fadwen – Glyndyfrdwy

Route: A gentle climb through pasture, woodland and
                 moorland to 414 metres on the western slopes
                 of Llantysilio Mountain is followed by an easy
                 descent along lanes to Glyndyfrdwy station.
Start: Llangollen Railway, Carrog Station.
Finish: Glyndyfrdwy Station.
Facilities: Tea room and toilets at Carrog station.
                 Campsite nearby. Pub in Carrog village.
                 Seasonal tea room and toilets at Glyndyfrdwy
                 station.
Time: 4-4½ hours.
OS Maps: 1:50 000 Landranger 125 and 116;
                 1:25 000 Explorer 255.

Carrog was originally a small hamlet known as Llansantffraid
Glyndyfrdwy. When the railway arrived in the 1860s, the name
was changed to Carrog, the name of a nearby farm, to give
tourists an easier name to pronounce! Sited in an attractive
location on Afon Dyfrdwy, the village grew in size as wealthy
Victorian and Edwardian families from Merseyside built
holiday homes along the riverside. Today, the tall buildings
present a picturesque scene when viewed from the 17th century
five-arched stone bridge spanning the river. Dedicated to St
Ffraid, a 6th century saint, the original village church was
swept away in a flood during 1601. A new church was built
higher up the hillside. Until demolished by the council, there
was a 14th century stone house in the village called Cachardy
Owain in which Owain Glyndŵr reputedly imprisoned his
enemies.

Walk Directions:

1. From Carrog station, walk out to the road and turn right. Cross the bridge over Afon Dyfrdwy (the River Dee) and bear left. Immediately after passing the Grouse Inn, turn right and follow a footpath uphill.

2. The path bends left then right to reach a stile. Continue ahead beside a fence along the edge of woodland. Shortly after the fence bends left, cross a stile and walk uphill through the field. When the fence on your right starts to descend, bear left to a stile.

3. Cross this large field by walking half-right to a stile in the far right corner. Continue ahead beside a wall and veer slightly right to cross a stone stile next to a gate.

4. Walk ahead on a wide enclosed track, crossing several stiles. In just under a kilometre, you will pass ruined farm buildings. Further on, the track passes through a field followed by another section of enclosed track. After entering another field, follow the left-hand fence but when it bends sharp left, walk gently downhill to a stile and gate in the far corner.

5. Emerge on a lane and turn right. In about 40 metres, where there is a lane on the left, bear right through a field gate. Follow a grassy track through gorse. After about 300 metres veer left to follow an old wall boundary on your left. Follow it around a corner then bear half-right to a broad gate.

6. Veer slightly left to follow a fence and wall along the edge of moorland. Go through a gate and continue along the bridleway. Cross a stream and follow the left-hand fence to another gate. In approximately 300 metres, when there is a gate leading into a narrow field on the left, bear right on a path that goes directly uphill, curving slightly to the right.

7. It becomes clearer and wider and in about 400 metres it bends left to emerge on a lane that crosses the side of Llantysilio Mountain. Turn right uphill to reach the highest point of the road in about 300 metres.

8. Continue along this scenic road as it descends with ever-changing views. Ignore a lane on the left and others on the right and left near a cattle grid.

9. After following the lane downhill for about 3.5 kilometres you will arrive at a lane junction in the Dee Valley. Turn left for about 500 metres then bear right to cross a bridge over the river. Follow the lane to Glyndyfrdwy station.

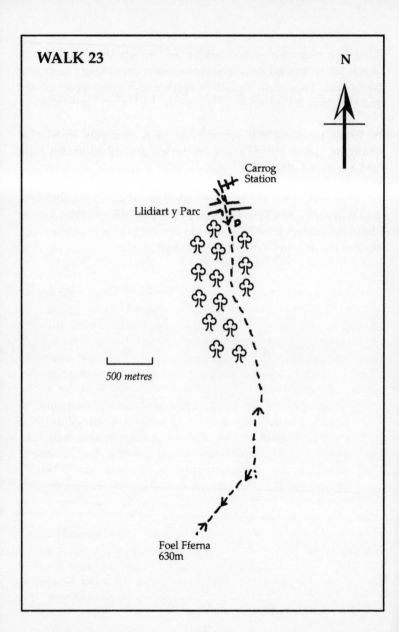

WALK 23

N

Carrog Station

Llidiart y Parc

500 metres

Foel Fferna
630m

Walk 23

5½ miles (9 kilometres)

Carrog – Llidiart y Parc – Moel Fferna – Carrog

Route: A gradual climb through forest and moorland to the Berwyn summit of Moel Fferna (630 m.). Return by the same route.

Start/Finish: Llangollen Railway, Carrog Station.

Facilities: Tea room and toilets at Carrog Station. Campsite nearby. Pub in Carrog village.

Time: 4-4½ hours.

OS Maps: 1:50 000 Landranger 125;
                 1:25 000 Explorer 255.

On the south side of Afon Dyfrdwy (the River Dee), a kilometre east of Llidiart y Parc, lies a tree covered motte known as Owain Glyndŵr's Mound. Thought to be originally the site of a Norman castle, it later became part of the Glyndyfrdwy estate, the ancestral home of Owain Glyndŵr. A moated mansion stood in a field adjacent to the mound. A descendant of the Princes of Powys and Deheubarth, Owain inherited the estate when his father died. He studied law and trained as a soldier. When Lord Grey of Rhuthun claimed land to which Glyndŵr's rights were dismissed, he gathered supporters against injustice. After meeting at Glyndŵr's house near Carrog, they attacked Rhuthun on fair day in September 1400. The war was to last 15 years during which Glyndŵr held parliament at Pennal and Machynlleth. His support gradually waned and there is no certainty as to where or how he ended his days.

From Llidiart y Parc, Moel Fferna is a straightforward climb through forest and moorland. From the summit looking north are superb views of the Clwydian hills. A few kilometres south are the highest peaks of the Berwyn range – Cadair Bronwen, Cadair Berwyn and Moel Sych. Closer is Ffordd Saeson, the

Englishmen's road, along which Henry II's army retreated in 1165 after being defeated by Owain Gwynedd.

Walk Directions:

1. From Carrog station walk out to the lane and turn left. On reaching the A5 at Llidiart y Parc, cross the road directly to a lane and follow it uphill. Ignore a footpath on the right. Pass a house on the left and continue ahead into forest. About 100 metres beyond the house, take a waymarked footpath on the left into trees. It goes uphill to meet a track.

2. Bear right and, in a few paces, go left on a path up a steep banking to meet the track again. Turn right along it for about 20 metres then bear left on a path. Ignore paths off it and maintain your direction, uphill. Pass a fenced grouse breeding area on the right and emerge on a forest track. Turn right and in about 30 metres bear left on another track.

3. Continue uphill along this track and pass fields on the left. Go through a gate across the track and walk ahead along the main track. Ignore a left-hand fork and bear right in a few paces, then left uphill through heather and bilberry moorland. In just over a kilometre, ignore a vague track on the right and, in a few paces, other tracks on the left. In approximately another 80 metres, leave the main track for a path on the right that goes directly up Moel Fferna.

4. The path may be vague at first but improves higher up. On the summit (630m) you will find a large cairn. In clear conditions, you will be rewarded with fine views of the Berwyn range. To return to Carrog, retrace your steps.

Rheilffordd Llyn Tegid (Bala Lake Railway)

Rheilffordd Llyn Tegid is built on a section of line that ran from Rhiwabon to Dolgellau and on to Barmouth Junction (Morfa Mawddach). The line to Dolgellau was run by four independent railways, these being the Vale of Llangollen, the Llangollen and Corwen, the Corwen and Bala and the Bala and Dolgellau. At Dolgellau there was a connection with the Cambrian branch that ran from Barmouth Junction. By 1896 the Great Western Railway had taken over the companies as far as Dolgellau. Declining profits in the mid 20th century led to Beeching's recommendation to close the line.

Local people realised the potential in preserving parts of the line, especially the picturesque section alongside Llyn Tegid. In 1971, six years after the line's closure, a public meeting in Bala led to the incorporation of a private company. Called Rheilffordd Llyn Tegid Cyf. (Bala Lake Railway Company) it was the first railway company to be registered entirely in the Welsh language.

A 1ft 11½inch (597mm) gauge line was laid on the old track bed and by 1976 the line was open from Llanuwchllyn to Y Bala. The main station and loco sheds are at Llanuwchllyn. Locomotive *Holy War* is a 0-4-0 saddle tank built by Hunslet of Leeds in 1902-3 for shunting at the Dinorwig slate quarry, Llanberis. *Maid Marian* operated on the Llanberis Lake Railway before coming to Y Bala.

Trains operate from April to the end of September and run every day in July and August. At the beginning and end of the season – apart from Bank Holidays – there are no trains on Mondays and Fridays.

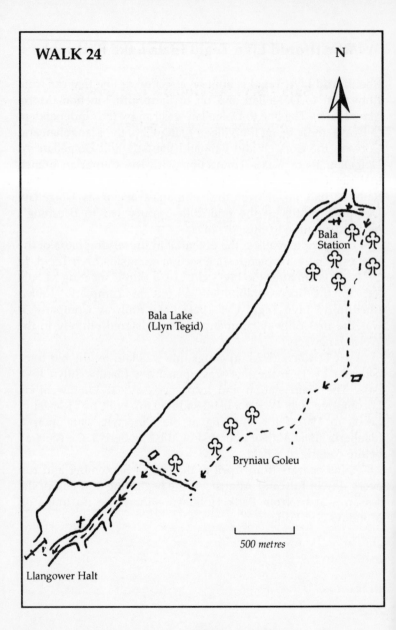

WALK 24

N

Bala Station

Bala Lake
(Llyn Tegid)

Bryniau Goleu

500 metres

Llangower Halt

Y Bala – Bryniau Golau – Llangower

Route:	Woodland and hillside paths above Llyn Tegid.
Start:	Rheilffordd Llyn Tegid, Bala Station.
Finish:	Llangower Halt.
Facilities:	Full facilities in Y Bala. Picnic area and public toilets near Llangower Halt.
Time:	2½ hours.
OS Maps:	1:50 000 Landranger 125;
	1:25 000 Outdoor Leisure 23.

Four miles long, Llyn Tegid (Bala Lake) is the largest natural lake in Wales. From the north eastern end, near the town of Y Bala, are fine views towards Aran Benllyn. A Site of Special Scientific Interest, the lake and its shores are a haven for wildlife as well as being popular with water sports enthusiasts. According to legend, the lake came into being when a cruel, sadistic prince was avenged for his wrong doings. One night, during a banquet, his palace and township were drowned. According to another story, Afon Dyfrdwy (the River Dee) flows through the lake without the waters mingling. The name Tegid probably comes from Tegid Foel, a 5th century Lord of Penllyn. The area of Penllyn includes the parishes of Llanuwchllyn, Llangower, Llandderfel, Llanfor and Llanycil.

After the invasion by the English under Edward I, Penllyn became part of the new county of Merionnydd. Around 1310 Roger de Mortimer made Y Bala an administrative centre and also rebuilt the streets to a grid system. A charter was granted and in 1324 the town became a free borough with a weekly market and two fairs. In the 18th and 19th centuries, Y Bala prospered as a centre for knitted stockings and gloves. George III was one of the customers. During this period, Y Bala became known for its preaching festivals and a Methodist college was established in the town. Thomas Charles, whose statue stands in Tegid Street, organized a system of Sunday schools and helped the spread of Bibles through the British and Foreign Bible Society. Sixteen year old Mary Jones walked from Llanfihangel-y-Pennant to buy a Bible from him in 1800. A Congregational minister of Y Bala, Michael D. Jones, was responsible for establishing the community of Welsh emigrants in Patagonia, South America in 1865. In Y Bala's High Street there is a statue of Thomas Ellis, Liberal MP for Meirionnydd in the 1890s. He was given the post of Chief Whip.

Walk Directions:

1. From Bala Station, walk out to the road and turn right. Ignore the road on the left and bear right again along the B4391. Pass the entrance to a caravan park and at the end of the grounds, turn right along a track.

2. In about 100 metres, turn left on a footpath that climbs through the forest. It meets a track at a bend. Bear left for 10 metres then climb the banking on the left to follow a clear path through coniferous trees to a stile.

3. Veer left uphill in the field to a fence. Follow it uphill to a corner and bear left beside it to a stile. Cross the field diagonally right to a corner stile. Walk beside the right hand fence to another stile and go ahead through gorse. Cross a ladder stile to the right of a house.

4. Join a track and turn right through an area of felled trees. Ignore a track on the left. Further on, take a waymarked path on the left and follow it to a track. Continue uphill to a stile. Walk ahead through the field and in 100 metres cross a stile on the right. Slant to the left downhill for about 150 metres to a stile in the descending fence.

5. Walk ahead on a path along Bryniau Golau hillside. As you descend gradually and cross a stream, there are wide views of Llyn Tegid. In about 600 metres the path reaches a fence. Continue beside it and ignore a gate into the woods. In 400 metres, near a sheepfold, cross a ladder stile.

6. Bear right to have a stream on your left. Go through some trees and, after crossing another stile, continue beside the stream. Climb a ladder stile on the left and cross a bridge to a footpath signpost. Walk ahead with a fence on the left and follow an old track.

7. Cross a ladder stile and turn left along the B4403. Ignore a road on the left and cross a bridge. Pass the church and follow the B4403 for about another 150 metres to a car park on the right. From the entrance, bear right towards the picnic area then go through a gate on the left to Llangower Halt and Llyn Tegid.

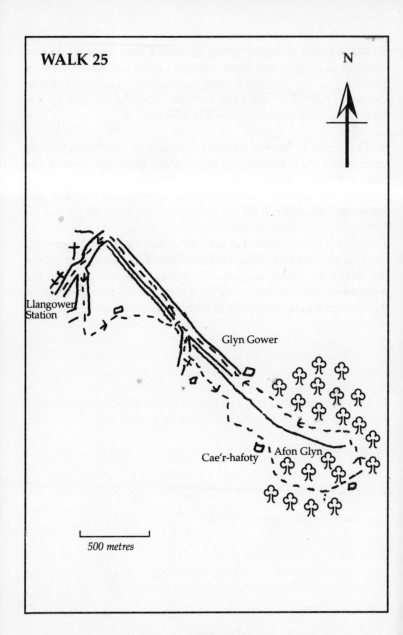

WALK 25

N

Llangower
Station

Glyn Gower

Cae'r-hafoty

Afon Glyn

500 metres

Llangower – Cae'r-hafoty – Glyn Gower – Llangower

Route: A long but gentle climb on paths and tracks
                  through pasture and forest. The descent is
                  along tracks and lanes through Glyn Gower.
Start/Finish: Bala Lake Railway, Llangower Halt.
Facilities: Picnic area and public toilets near the start.
Time: 3-3½ hours.
OS Maps: 1:50 000 Landranger 125;
                  1:25 000 Outdoor Leisure 23.

Llangower is the only village on Rheilffordd Llyn Tegid
between the stations of Llanuwchllyn and Bala. The 18th
century church contains an unusual wheel-less funeral bier
which was carried by having a horse at each end. Situated
halfway along Llyn Tegid, Llangower halt is ideally located for
picnics or watching birds. Herons, cormorants, ducks, grebes
and other species may be spotted. Found nowhere else in
Britain and possibly trapped here since the last Ice Age, a fish
known as the *gwyniad* inhabits the depths of the lake.

Walk Directions:

1. From Llangower halt platform, walk out to the lane and turn
left. In about 200 metres, turn right on a lane opposite the
church. Pass a drive to Tŷ Cerrig and, where the lane bends
right at a stream, cross a stile near a gate on your left.

2. Walk uphill with the stream on your left. Go through a gap
in a fence to enter another field and immediately go left
downhill to a stile. Cross the small footbridge and take the path

ahead, uphill. Do not take a path on the left that follows a fence but walk beside an old field boundary that has a few trees alongside it.

3. Cross a ladder stile and bear slightly left downhill. Pass farm buildings on your left and bear right to cross two ladder stiles a few meters apart. Follow a fence on your left and, after crossing another stile, continue along a track bordered by trees. Go downhill to a stile and walk on to meet a forest track.

4. Turn left to cross a bridge over Afon Glyn and go through a gate. Walk up to the lane and turn right. Ignore a lane on the left and cross the river again. In about another 50 metres, where the lane bends right, walk ahead along a track to pass a converted chapel on your right. Continue along a grassy track with the river and forest on your left.

5. Follow the track around to the right. When approaching a cottage on the right, bear left away from it to have a field boundary on the right. On reaching a fence directly ahead, bear slightly right uphill (look back for fine views). In about 200 metres veer left with the track to go through a gate opening and follow the track to the buildings of Cae'r-hafoty.

6. Pass Cae'r-hafoty on your right and bear right to find an old track bordered by trees. Follow it through an old field boundary then veer half left beside a line of trees. Cross a damp area to another line of trees and walk ahead to a gap in a fence. Turn left to cross a stile at the edge of the forest.

7. Veer slightly right on a path through heather and coniferous trees. In almost 400 metres, at a footpath and bridleway junction, bear left beside an area of felled forest. Cross a stream and continue ahead to some ruins. Walk between the ruined buildings and pass an old cottage.

8. Join a better track and bear left downhill to emerge on a forest track. Turn left and, in 100 metres, ignore a bridleway on the right. In a few more metres, at a junction of tracks, go left downhill.

9. The track crosses a stream and becomes surfaced as it descends through Glyn Gower. In about 1.5 kilometres it emerges on the lane walked earlier. Bear right and either cross the bridge to retrace your steps over the hill, or follow the lane to the B4403. Turn left for approximately 400 metres to Llangower halt.

Welshpool and Llanfair Railway

The 2ft 6inch (762mm) railway opened in 1903 to link Llanfair Caereinion with the main line at Welshpool (Y Trallwng). At first owned by the Welshpool and Llanfair Light Railway Company and operated by the Cambrian Railway, it was taken over by the Great Western Railway. Mainly because of the local bus service introduced by G.W.R. in 1925, the passenger trains were not well used and ceased in 1931. Freight trains continued until 1956.

Within a few weeks of the railway's closure, a preservation society was formed which was later replaced by the Welshpool and Llanfair Light Railway Preservation Company. Operations were based at Llanfair Caereinion and, although the first section of 7 km (4½ miles) to Castle Caereinion was soon cleared, extensive work was needed further along the line and the terminus at Raven's Square Welshpool did not open until 1981. The eight mile line climbs steep gradients on its journey into the Banw valley.

Trains are hauled by massive locomotives with faraway backgrounds. Built in France in 1944, *Sir Drefaldwyn* (no. 10) operated in Austria. No. 14 was built by Hunslet of Leeds in 1954 for Sierra Leone Railways. Several of the coaches were built in 1900-1 for the Zillertalbahn in Austria whilst others are bogie saloon coaches from Africa.

Trains operate from April until late October. At Easter, school half-terms (not February) and mid-July to the end of August, they run everyday. In June, early July and early September trains operate everyday except Mondays and Fridays. At the beginning and end of the season, trains run at weekends only.

Llanfair Caereinion

Route:	Town, riverside and woodland walk.
Start/Finish:	Welshpool and Llanfair Railway, Llanfair Caereinion Station.
Facilities:	Refreshments and toilets at the start. Pubs in the town.
Time:	1½-2 hours.
OS Maps:	1:50 000 Landranger 125; 1:25 000 Explorer 215.

Llanfair Caereinion is a tranquil, small market town standing beside Afon Banw. The Romans had a fort here, to the south on Gibbet Hill. Stage coaches stopped in the town on the journey between Shrewsbury and Aberystwyth, bringing trade to the shops and inns. In 1758 there was a great fire and many of the thatched buildings were burnt down. Behind the church of St Mary is Ffynnon Fair, a pre-Christian well believed to have healing properties, and used for such purposes until the early 20th century. Outside the porch of the church is a sundial on a marble plinth. Although rebuilt in 1868, the church retains some earlier features, including the effigy of a knight, Dafydd ap Gruffudd Fychan.

Beside the river is the Goat Field Arboretum with its twenty-five species of native trees. Further on is Deri Woods with its Interpretative Centre in an old pump house, and the Gorsedd Stones. Passed on the walk, in a clearing of the arboretum, stands the wooden sculpture which tells the story of Taliesin, son of Ceridwen. He was born after Gwion Bach, son of Gwreag of Llanfair Caereinion accidentally swallowed Ceridwen's magic potion. Although Gwion changed his form several times to evade capture by Ceridwen, she also changed and, as a grain

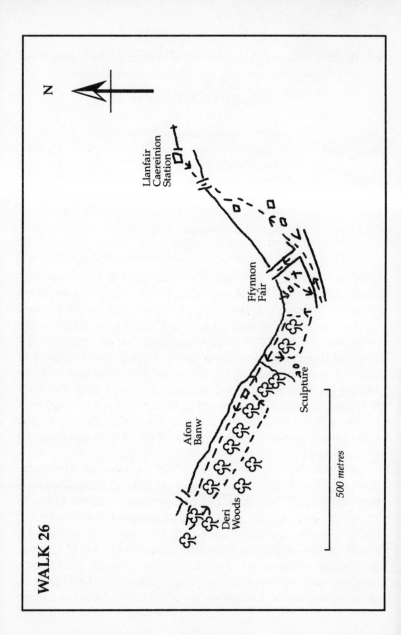

WALK 26

Llanfair
Caereinion Station

Ffynnon
Fair

Afon
Banw

Deri
Woods

Sculpture

500 metres

N

of wheat he was eaten by her when she became a hen. Nine months later, she bore a handsome son, Taliesin. In the churchyard wall, near the Moriah Chapel, is a slate sculpture to Taliesin.

Walk Directions:

1. From the station, cross a road and a footbridge over Afon Banw. Follow the road to houses and turn left. Shortly bear right and, in a few metres, bear right along a tarmac path. On reaching a road, turn left to pass The Black Lion on your left.

2. At crossroads, turn right down Bridge Street. Immediately after passing the Institute (a black and white building) turn left on a surfaced path. Walk uphill to St Mary's Church and follow a path on your right to St Mary's Well. Another interesting feature in the churchyard is the sundial near the porch.

3. Follow the path to the road and turn right. In about 100 metres go through a kissing gate on the right. Take a path that bears right downhill to Afon Banw. Ignore footpaths on the left and follow the path to the Interpretative Centre at a view point near the river.

4. Continue along the footpath close to the river until you reach a footbridge over Afon Banw. Do not cross it, but walk on a few metres and bear left with the path. Ignore the path on the right, and continue along the level path with the river below on your left. At a junction turn left until you see a circle of stones (the Gorsedd Stones) in a clearing on your left.

5. Enter the clearing and bear left down steps to the Interpretative Centre. Turn right to cross a small bridge then bear right up steps to the wooden Taliesin sculpture in a small clearing.

6. On reaching another path, turn left and ignore all other paths on the left. Go through the kissing-gate and turn left. After passing St Mary's Church, retrace your steps past The Black Lion to the station.